DAILY INSIGHTS

The *Bowl of* SAKI

Hazrat Inayat Khan

Commentary By Murshid Samuel L. Lewis

Sufi Ruhaniat International • San Francisco • California

Sufi Ruhaniat International
410 Precita Avenue
San Francisco CA 94110
www.ruhaniat.org

ISBN 978-0-9881778-0-2
eISBN 978-0-9881778-1-9
Library of Congress Control Number: 2012947149

Second Edition

Book Design by Professor Nuria Stephanie Sabato

Introduction

"The Bowl of Saki," with its 366 aphorisms selected from the writings of Hazrat Inayat Khan, one for each day of the year, is a widely read and much appreciated text. Most people access it through various email lists and services. Many of these posts include the remarkable spiritual commentaries on these sayings written by Murshid Samuel L. Lewis, one of Hazrat Inayat Khan's foremost disciples, who was the originator of the Dances of Universal Peace, and the founder of the Sufi Ruhaniat International.

It is unfortunate that consideration of this work has up until this time mostly been confined to readers studying it as a kind of daily oracle. Since wisdom is always wisdom, one cannot get any bad advice from consulting "The Bowl of Saki" with its commentaries in this way. However, a reader who is looking for insight on the spiritual path and a practical and systematic approach to mystical realization should take a fresh look at this text, and consider it in a much broader way than has heretofore been done.

Three or four years ago, I happened to notice as I occasionally referred to the daily posting of this text that there were quite a few references in it to the nature and importance of the soul. As I often presented teachings on the Sufi view of the soul, I asked my esoteric secretary Tawwaba Bloch to extract all the sections that mentioned this word to facilitate using it in my classes. She did so, and Amrita Blaine, the Ruhaniat secretary at the time, gave it the title "Soul in the Bowl." This was a particularly apt title, as one of the teachings in the text is the Sufi metaphor of the Heart, the center of feeling, being like a globe within which the light of the soul manifests to the extent that the heart is clear of impressions that cloud its surface.

Later I came to see that it wasn't simply the soul that was deeply portrayed in this work, but so many of the core teachings of Sufism were presented in a very accessible and clear way. This realization added fuel to the fire of publishing a proper book of "The Bowl of Saki" with Murshid Samuel Lewis's commentaries so that it might be studied in a deeper way, not only by Sufi mureeds, but also by a wider audience.

This version of the text is the result. Consistent with modern usage, we thought it appropriate to make the English phraseology more gender inclusive. Inclusivity was certainly the intention of both Murshid Sam and Hazrat Inayat Khan, but the generally accepted grammatical usage of their time didn't have this form and relied solely on the masculine pronoun. Farrunnissa Rosa did a great deal of initial work toward gender inclusivity, and when I edited it further for publication, I continued her process. Boudewijn Boom also made a major contribution to the initial editing process by standardizing the spellings of Arabic and non-English words and ensuring consistent punctuation. Suria Rebecca McBride's assistance in proofing the final version was invaluable. For Hazrat Inayat Khan's quotes, we have retained the punctuation and capitalization used in the 1936 publication of "The Bowl of Saki."

Thanks to the tireless research and scholarship of Sharif Graham in perusing the archives of the Sufi Movement, we wish to acknowledge his finding that some of the sayings in "The Bowl of Saki" are not the actual words of Hazrat Inayat Khan, though they are inspired by his teachings. They come from compositions of two of his senior students, created as part of the "Voice of Inayat" series which is included in the Sufi Message volumes. The sayings for February 2 and for June 18-21 are from Murshida Sherifa Lucy Goodenough's "Love, Human and Divine," and the sayings for July 14-25 and for September 25-27 are from Mary Zohra Williams' "Pearls from an Ocean Unseen." We feel it appropriate to recognize their contributions.

We are especially grateful to Nuria Stephanie Sabato for her beautiful work in designing the cover for this new edition of "The Bowl of Saki" and for her dedicated professional creative attention to all the design elements in the text itself. It is very meaningful that several representatives of different lineages that trace themselves to Hazrat Inayat Khan all supported this project to offer his words for daily contemplation along with the commentaries of Murshid Samuel Lewis in an attractive and authentic way, along with our mutual prayer that the Message of God may spread far and wide, illuminating the whole of humanity.

As Murshid Samuel Lewis's esoteric secretary, I was often blessed by his transmission when he was writing his commentaries on his teacher's words. He would be in a state of attunement with Pir-o-Murshid Inayat Khan, and I would be attuned to him while taking dictation on a typewriter. It was a remarkable experience of catching the flow of guidance like a stream in awakened consciousness. Such experiences helped prepare me to edit his writings.

Murshid Sam wrote and rewrote his commentaries on the esoteric teachings and published writings of his teacher throughout his whole adult life. He never ceased receiving fresh inspiration from this study. His conscientiousness in this regard—as well as my own sense of confidence that I knew what he was trying to say—encouraged me in my editing process of this text to be willing to make a few changes in his form of expression to enhance clarity and to communicate more clearly to readers. I also occasionally took the liberty to add a phrase or two to make sure his main points would be properly understood.

There are quite a few philosophical terms that appear in Murshid Sam's commentaries, many of them from Arabic and Sanskrit, and occasionally Hebrew. If you are not familiar with them, don't let them put you off, as they are often almost always defined in the context of the paragraph or elsewhere in the text. The more important ones are repeated in different places throughout.

In particular, in his process of drawing out and applying some of the hidden meanings in Hazrat Inayat Khan's pithy sayings, Murshid Samuel Lewis often wrote about the importance of the Sufi practices of *Fikr*, *Zikr*, and *Darood*. Briefly defined, *Zikr* is the repetition of a sacred phrase, usually *la ilaha ilallahu*, which affirms the Unity of the One and Only Being, Allah, in remembrance. *Fikr* is the process of carrying this remembrance of God and God's divine qualities consciously, and often continuously, on the swing of the breath. And *Darood* is likewise a breath practice that carries the intention of leaving your notion of a separate self behind, focusing in a one-pointed way on the flow of the breath, moving ever "Toward the One," and continuously merging with the Oneness.

While this work is filled with beautiful philosophical teachings on the nature of mysticism and the spiritual path, you can be sure that both these great teachers would say that even a few experiences of piercing through the mind-mesh where human beings are caught up in the inherent conflict of the analytical mind, and touching the sphere of Universal Light-Life-Love, are worth more than all the intellectual content to be found within this text. The wonderful thing is that through meditating on the potent words of these Sufi teachers we are given very clear practical methods to do just this. The website MurshidSam.org, particularly the living voice archived there, is filled with blessings and is another resource for this discovery.

In the end, the overarching purpose of becoming what is meant by truly being a Sufi, a *Buzurg*, or a *Bodhisattva* stands forth. When this realization dawns, each one understands their intrinsic connection with all beings and lives a life of service toward awakening the true self in all. We are led to see how we are all interconnected in such a way that our thoughts, feelings, and realization affect the whole of creation. We thus become vehicles of joy, love, and wisdom so that all beings may overcome pain and suffering.

May you, dear reader, drink deeply of this Bowl of Saki, the cup of the wine of the presence of God, being offered you by these great souls, who through their inspiration have brought forth the nectar of the Spirit of Guidance.

Wali Ali Meyer
San Francisco 2012

January 1

As water in a fountain flows as one stream, but falls in many drops divided by time and space, so are the revelations of the one stream of truth.

Truth is the Universal Life which permeates and penetrates all things. It is the same as Universal Light called *Amida* by the Buddhists which should not be regarded as different from Allah or God. Any difference comes from the intervention of the mind-weaving. The Universal Light penetrating through the meshes of the mind reflects in forms through the world of limitation—that is to say, where there is time and where there is space.

If by cognition one means mental grasping, this is not the acquiring of truth. Truth can never be achieved by philosophy. It is only when the consciousness arises above time and space, that it perceives the Grand Unity beyond the mental realm. It is this that may be called Revelation, and no one who has ever experienced it will find its Essence contradictory to anyone else who has ever experienced it.

Sometimes the spiritual evolution of personality reaches such an exalted stage that the one is called *Avatar* or *Rassoul*. This is the result of rending the mind-mesh so that the Divine Light penetrates into the physical body, and the life of body, mind, and spirit is one. In such cases the words of the speaker are termed "Revelation," but the real revelation consists not of the words but of the personality and atmosphere of the Divine Messenger. As the Universal Light and Life are ever one and the same, and as the process of revelation always consists of this breaking through of the mind-mesh and the pouring of spiritual abundance upon the body, such experience can well be likened to the rising of a geyser or fountain, only in this case the depths of the spring are in the universal sphere.

January 2

All names and forms are the garbs and covers
under which the one life is hidden.

This Universal Life penetrates all things. It has two aspects, a rising and a falling, an expansion and a contraction. Through the heating of expansion in Love the Higher was formed; through the cooling of contraction in Beauty the Lower, or external, was formed. The waves of vibrations from these met and intermingled forming the mind-mesh where light and darkness both are found. The Universal Light falling between the meshes of mind upon the outer sphere gave rise to the myriads of forms which have been given names by humankind to distinguish them, but really the Essence is one and the same. Who understands this understands something of the Nature of Allah.

January 3

Truth without a veil is always uninteresting to the human mind.

Above this mind-mesh, the conflicting interplay of thoughts, there is a Universal condition which cannot be grasped by the human mind. Human beings can understand it through the heart faculty but not through the mind. Although mind was formed by the interplay of forces from the lower and upper worlds, and in this were the heavens, as well as the hells made from the earth, nevertheless, the Light of Intelligence shining through the mind-mesh from above causes mind to look below upon name and form.

Even when it looks up it does not see anything beyond this mesh which forms the sky of *Malakut*, the Mental Plane, even as a fish cannot see above the surface of the water. Personality on earth looks up only so far—the light is turned back toward earth, forming again between the Mental Plane and earth the Psychic Realm, which is created by human reflections and emotions. The Psychic Realm is not in reality a sphere such as the Physical Plane (*Nasut*), the Mental Plane (*Malakut*), and the Spiritual Plane (*Djabrut*). In reality it is subjective, formed by the mind turning in upon itself and its experiences.

The veil of Isis is this same sky of *Malakut*, and when once that is penetrated the Goddess is beheld in all Her Glory.

January 4

When you stand with your back to the sun, your shadow is before you;
but when you turn and face the sun, your shadow falls behind you.

This statement describes the difference between the average person and the illuminated soul. It is primarily a difference of will, not of capability. Average people, who are under the sway of external influence, permit their will to be deceived by the mind. They look down from above, like someone leaning over the wharf and gazing into the depths of the ocean. All they see are reflections and shadows. So they become caught in this web, which is nothing but the shadow of the vibrations interpenetrating in the mind-mesh.

When one turns to the path of God one begins to look upward. Therefore spiritual education is called a turning and a tuning. Then the shadow-thoughts and the shadow-words and the shadow-interests fade into nascence, and the whole attention is focused upon God and Unity. This is the meaning of the Sufi Invocation, "Toward the One, the Perfection of Love, Harmony, and Beauty, the Only Being; United with All the Illuminated Souls, Who form the Embodiment of the Master, the Spirit of Guidance."

January 5

No one has seen God and lived. To see God we must be non-existent.

It is the human mind which determines human existence. When one rises above the mind-mesh, existence continues but one does not. That is to say, the life in God is the non-existence of human life. So long as we exist as self we remain below the mind-mesh; in the life above the mind-mesh there is no self as we understand it.

January 6

The truth cannot be spoken; that which can be spoken is not the truth.

Truth is an Absolute, Transcendent Unity. Sounds are created out of Sound by the Universal Sound (called *Logos* by the Christians) which penetrates the mind-mesh giving rise to all particular sounds. Particular sounds show the existence of Universal Sound but do not explain it.

Universal Truth is Universal Sound and not Silence. It is active, it is Life, yet in a certain sense it is changeless above and includes all change. Human speech comes into existence by the grasping of the rays of Universal Sound by the mind-mesh, but none of such utterances can either be or describe the Universal Sound which is Truth. A chicken cannot be described by the eggs she hatches, yet it is natural for the chicken to lay eggs. Even so, human speech, through the praising of God, causes a turning back to God. This happens through the process of renunciation (not abolition) of thought and speech. Through such a process we become one with Truth, and Truth is reflected in speech. Truth is the cause of speech but of itself it is not speech.

January 7

The only power for the mystic is the power of love.

This has two explanations: There is one Power in the Universe, and that Power is Love. This one Power is that Universal Energy which we have been calling Life or Light. This is only a naming of it; it is not a description of it. It is this same Power which gave rise to the Universe producing the positive and negative vibrations and atoms which directly or indirectly gave rise to all planes and all forms.

Now what is or was this Power? It is the Power which comes from letting go, from losing the self, the Power which arises from non-attachment to personality. And that is nothing but Love. God so loved, that God created. And God so loved the world that was created that God permitted this Power to appear in fullness in a human being. Such is the mystery of Christhood, that gave everyone the opportunity first to witness, and then through example to attain to, the fullness of this Power of Love while in the human body in the physical world. This was the very purpose of creation.

January 8

If people but knew their own religion, how tolerant they would become, and how free from any grudge against the religion of others.

What is this knowledge of religion? In its fullest sense it is nothing but knowledge of God, the One, the Only Being. Without knowledge of God there can be no knowledge of religion. There may be belief in religion but there is not knowledge of religion. Until there has been the personal experience and contact such that the mind has grasped its significance, it cannot be called knowledge. When another has learned it, it is not one's own knowledge. But when it has become part of one's own life, it is one's knowledge.

Now this knowledge of God, how does it bring tolerance? It brings tolerance because it makes one see all and know all. If it does not make one see all and know all it is not knowledge of God.

The God of popular religion is that name given to the human thought-concept of Divinity, but that human thought-concept is not the Reality. God is the Reality which, when apprehended, causes this condition of universal beneficence and compassion toward all creatures. That is why Allah is called *Er-Rahman, Er-Rahim,* infinite compassion, infinite mercy.

January 9

The real meaning of crucifixion is to crucify the false self, that the true self may rise. As long as the false self is not crucified, the true self is not realized.

The Cross is the symbol of Light. The vertical line is the way by which Light passes from Source to manifestation and also the way by which energy returns from manifestation to Source. This is seen in the breath. The horizontal line is caused by the action between the lower and upper currents and forms the mind-mesh.

The Cross has two forms, one like the letter "T" in the European languages. This represents the crucifixion of the soul in matter. The energy does not pass above the horizontal line. It strikes it and returns again to the earth-plane. This action is called Karma, and it brings to one the results of all speech, thought, and action.

The teaching of all sages was to rise above this Karma. That brought the upper part of the vertical line of the Cross. It is that portion which is the Divine Light. But one cannot carry anything through the close lines of the mind-mesh. Only light will go through. Not only are all passions and sentiments too coarse to pass through and above it to the Buddhic Condition (*Nuri Mohammed*), but even good thoughts and feelings cannot pass. Nothing can pass but thought and feeling of Unity, which is called Love, and this is the very essence of Soul.

By this process the false self is crucified and left behind. What is the false self? It is nothing but the thought of self made into a falsified reality, a pseudo-sun in the mental world. When one perceives the true Light this sun disappears. Or, by ignoring this false sun, one perceives the true sun. This is the higher crucifixion, and in the case of Jesus Christ and Moses and some others, it even caused the disintegration of the physical body, which had been kept together by the thought-form of the personality. When thought became completely immersed in God, even the physical body disintegrated. That is *Parinirvana* when even matter is spiritualized.

January 10

An ideal is beyond explanation. To analyze God is to dethrone God.

The realm of Ideals, or what Plato called Ideas, exists above the mind-mesh. The Divine Light striking the realm of Ideals is partly refracted, and then reflected above the mind-mesh. This produces the Ideas in the realm of Pure Light, so that their Nature is Light; also they are purely God, taking on what might be called the Intelligent Aspect of God.

As human mind does not and cannot reach this plane, it is impossible to express the condition there in human thought and in human words. These arise below the mind-mesh. Besides, what we call exposition or analysis is of the nature of distinction; things are known by how and to what extent they differ. The spiritual Ideas are not differentiated in this way.

By the same token, all that is above the mental *Akasha* is God, whether it is explained or described or referred to in various manners and by different words. Nevertheless, these words do not really bring one any knowledge; they are symbols which indicate there are different conditions, but as all these conditions are above and beyond the human mind and larger than the human mind in scope, they are no more intelligible to it than the ocean would be to a cup.

JANUARY 15

Yes, teach your principles of good, but do not think to limit God within them.
The goodness of each of us is peculiar to ourselves.

For what we call "good" comes from the favorable effects caused beneath the mind-mesh. Consequently, it is our name, our thought, and not the lasting Divine Thought that actually gives them life. God is the Essence of all Qualities and is not affected by our thought upon any quality.

JANUARY 16

To learn to adopt the standard of God, and to cease to wish to make the world
conform to one's own standard of good, is the chief lesson of religion.

Prayer is a good thing; praying "Thy will be done" is always helpful, but one also must act in such a way that the prayer becomes a reality. This is the fulfillment of prayer. To pray and then leave the matter to fate is to experience the desire of the prayer without the desired or beneficial results.

Real prayer is to attune one's whole being so that the Divine Light may bring about the fulfillment of prayer. This can only be done when one ceases to place any obstacle in the path of the prayer. When thought-force or logic are applied to prayer, the wish—and the breath which starts to take that wish to Heaven—is caught in the mind-mesh and either does not return, or returns in a form not always acceptable or good. This has led some people to deny the efficacy of prayer, but really what they are denying is not prayer because as soon as mental obstacles obtrude in the path of that prayer, it cannot reach Heaven, cannot touch the ear of God.

It is by mental conformation, by keeping the heart pure, and controlling mind by will that one is enabled both to reach God and also to receive from God. This identifies the most desirable life and religion. When one is given the strength and inspiration to accomplish or cooperate in the accomplishment of the desire of prayer it is the highest successful fulfillment of prayer. This is done by keeping one's feelings in an awakened condition, above the mental net of *samsara*.

January 17

Thought draws the line of fate.

This is true not only in prayer but in all things. Every exhalation sends something out, and every inhalation draws something in. That which is expelled carries a message, as a flying dove going upward. As soon as another thought is received into the mind, it impedes the upward journey of that breath-message. When any act, thought, speech, or desire strikes the mind-mesh, it is propelled downward toward the earth plane and brings with it the results of a movement which is at the same time personal and individual, and also cosmic, in the sense that the whole sphere endeavors to keep its balance and sends back the compensatory vibrations to those sent out by us.

To overcome this action, *Fikr* is practiced in some form. In daily *Fikr* or *Darood*, when a thought is accompanied by a Divine Breath it can automatically arise through the meshes of the mental net and pass through *Djabrut* to the *Arsh*, the throne of God. That is to say, the automatic wish of the average person can rise no higher than the thought or will behind it, but for the spiritual person, the initiate, whose thought and desire are accompanied by *Darood*, these automatically rise above the mental world into the empyrean unless another thought deliberately interferes. Practice of concentration with *Fikr* perfects this process.

January 18

Misbelief alone misleads; single-mindedness always leads to the goal.

By misbelief is not meant wrong belief. Any human belief can be called right and any belief can be called wrong. Misbelief therefore does not mean wrong belief but belief that does not carry itself through clearly to the subject of the belief. That is because even when thoroughly believing, mind entertains an unconscious doubt or insufficient knowledge.

A strong concentration throws ample light on the belief and rights it. That is to say, it permits the Light of God's Intelligence to fall upon it. This enables one to hold or express beliefs or opinions which are in harmony with Cosmic Truth, that is to say, with the Will of God.

January 19

A monarch is ever a monarch,
whether crowned with a jeweled crown or clad in beggar's garb.

This may be paraphrased as "Ruler is one who is ruler over oneself." No one can be called a monarch whose subjects do not obey. Who and what are the subjects of the monarch? They are not only the personalities who give real or pretended obeisance; they include the thoughts and passions of the personality and one's real or potential control over affairs.

Thought-concentration on a monarch, or by a monarch over his or her dominion, subtly connects the breath with the affairs of the domain. This means that there is a strong karmic link between all movements, inner or outer, of the monarch, and those of the domain. This is true for every individual, free or slave, whether one bows to another, has others bow to one, or neither bows or is bowed before.

January 20

To treat every human being as a shrine of God is to fulfill all religion.

Religion being the tie between the devotee and God, if such a one does not see—actually see—God everywhere, he or she has not come to the fulfillment of love. This is not a philosophy, it is a reality. It is seen and known.

God may be respected by treating our human kin as brothers and sisters in the Divine Parenthood. This is one step and is called Morals. But there is a higher step which is to see God alone as the very life under all names and forms. This may be called Knowledge and it may be called Love. If one has not this feeling it will grow automatically by practice of *Fikr* and *Darood*.

January 21

The wise should keep the balance between love and power;
one should keep the love in one's nature ever increasing and expanding,
and at the same time strengthen the will so that the heart may not easily be broken.

Power is what God gives naturally to us, and love is what we should give naturally to God. Power enters with every breath. This can easily be demonstrated without any knowledge of metaphysics, for the person who does not breathe will surely lose the connection between the physical body and the subtle bodies and pass from form. It is the use of breath which can be the most valuable thing in life.

If the body tries to collect power and express power without love, it will be like a balloon bag being filled with gas. It has only a certain capacity and to exert it beyond that capacity will cause damage or destruction. Likewise the love for God which is unbalanced, which makes one mad with love or fervent with devotion does not give God the opportunity to use the pious person as a Divine Instrument. God wants to express Divine Power through the pure vehicle and the person has not made the vehicle ready. This shows weakness of will even in the midst of love, which is intoxicating.

Will is strengthened by keeping the balance between power and love which are both aspects of will. *Urouj* and *Nasoul*, inhalation and exhalation, the upward and downward currents, must be kept in balance and rhythm in order to secure maximum efficiency. If there is too much power, even the physical heart will be strained; if there is too much love, it will experience pleasure and pain, ecstasy and suffering. But if the love is ever expanding, ever growing, and made sober by the desire to do God's Will, then the person will also be a receptacle of power expressed or concealed. Even the gentlest saint may be a most majestic person through the attunement of will and breath to God.

January 22

Failure comes when will surrenders to reason.

Will is the Divine Energy which penetrates the mind-mesh and has capacity to rise above it. When the mind begins to turn its thought upon particular experiences, it seizes the will-power and prevents it from returning to God, keeping it in the mind. This is the murder of Abel by Cain. This causes all suffering and also prevents further will-power from entering the sphere. Mind cannot use that beyond its capacity but can misuse anything and everything.

The great weakness in reason is that every person may use it for some particular end, and even wickedness can be defended by an argumentative mind.

JANUARY 23

Success comes when reason, the store of experience, surrenders to will.

This is a natural process. The first movement of will is a downward current from Allah, through the heavens, to earth. This downward current pulls other things with it. It attracts other vibrations and collects them on the physical plane. If the will is not hampered on its return journey to God, it can descend again and bring more. This rise and fall of will is the Power and Love of God expressed through the Cosmic breath. It operates automatically through *Fikr* and *Darood* and in that way they are the greatest aids to concentration.

Concentration collects the mental atoms but only keeps them in place when feeling controls thought. If this is persisted in, it will sooner or later force an accommodation in the physical sphere. This is success. So you see success is a positive action of will, while failure and evil are both due to weakness. Even from the selfish point of view selflessness proves to be the highest and best form of selfishness.

JANUARY 24

There is an answer to every call; those who call on God, to them God comes.

Jesus Christ has said, "Not every one who saith 'Lord, Lord' will enter the kingdom of Heaven, but he that doeth the Will of the Father." This is very important and a mighty teaching. To call upon God one not only needs to use a Name of God—or the Name may be dispensed with under certain conditions—but other names, thoughts, and desires must be rejected at that time.

Nevertheless, every call, whether expressed in speech or thought, rises to its proper sphere and returns to earth. If it is confined to the karmic sphere, it brings its natural fruit, but if it is united to pure will, it brings something Divine. So the speech or prayer to God, not coupled with any thought, feeling, or emotion which would return to the *nufs*, reaches God.

This does not bring God to one since God is already there, but it enables the person to recognize and realize God and to serve God so that God's success and one's own success are one.

JANUARY 25

A person who thinks against their own desire is their own enemy.

Once a thought or wish is released, its effect is influenced most by the original thinker, who is always attuned to it. If such a one says or thinks something against it, it immediately reaches the mental plane on the breath and destroys all the concentration that has been set up there. Without an accommodation being made on the mental plane, there can be no success on the physical plane. This is a wonderful law which makes us the master of our own destiny, and gives us what is erroneously called freedom of will, but which is, strictly speaking, continuous opportunity to do good, no matter how many the shortcomings or how often the repetition of serious mistakes. That is to say, the Mercy and Forgiveness of God are characterized by the Wisdom which enables one to **see**, not by any blind relief from mistakes. But neither is one punished other than in one's failure to succeed until one understands and practices the Law—mental, moral, or spiritual.

JANUARY 26

The brain speaks through words; the heart in the glance of the eyes; and the soul through a radiance that charges the atmosphere, magnetizing all.

In the explanation of the idea of *Logos* included particularly in the Christian religion, it has been forgotten that each word or doctrine has three discrete interpretations according to the **degree of understanding** and according to the **plane of application**. Really these two mean the same thing, for accordingly as the understanding is expanded, so will the more subtle plane be contacted.

However, when people lost the power and ability to contact the higher sphere, the mind began to consider the manifestations of three *Logoi*, as if they were all separate, and spoke of the Triune God. This trinity has no reality except in the human mind; at the same time it is a very real thought and arises from the natural tendency of the human mind to analyze. And so it can be said at the same time that God is Triune, yet in the absolute sense God can be, and is nothing but, Unity above all explanations.

Mentally interpreted, *Logos* means word, or perhaps reason or doctrine. The brain, as the delegate of mind, expresses physically through words. But on the heart plane, *Logos* means Light and Law (Latin *lex*, *legis*) and one can see the resemblance between these words showing that they came from one root. The actual root was this Divine Light as expressed in the mental plane. Jesus Christ said, "The light of the body is in the eye," so that Divine Light from the heart plane, passing through the mental plane is divulged in the physical eye.

But while *Logos* means word or thought or reason or doctrine mentally, and Light or Law spiritually, it is also true as the Bible teaches, that first was the *Logos*, and the *Logos* was with God and the *Logos* was God. The *Logos* was in the very beginning with God. That is to say that *Logos* was and is the very emanation from the *Arsh*-throne of God and is this universal Power-Love ocean-stream of vibrations.

Emanation individualized is called *Ruh*, or soul, by the Sufis, but it is nevertheless one with this Universal Ocean of Love, and when vivified cannot be confined to any part of the human personality. So when the soul awakens, this energy magnetizes the complete atmosphere of the person, and even a much greater area around one.

JANUARY 27

Love is the merchandise which all the world demands;
if you store it in your heart, every soul will become your customer.

The first explanation of this is that there is no explanation, as Love is its own explanation. Also it is self-explanatory, and without this Love nothing conveyed to the mind will clarify it. At the same time the mind cannot be thoroughly efficient without it. Concentration cannot be accomplished without feeling, without power. When the concentration takes one into this Universal Ocean of Love, it is found to be the essence of the heart stream. Then everything and everybody will be attracted. This living evidence is the only clarification.

January 28

Sincerity is the jewel that forms in the shell of the heart.

This being a condition of the heart, mind cannot grasp it. It is one of those truths which have to be posited without being explained. To test it in one way is to enter *Darood*, or better yet, *Fikr*, and to breathe concentrating on sincerity. You will find it in the heart. Or concentrate on the heart as you breathe and you will find sincerity at its very core.

January 29

Self-pity is the worst poverty; it overwhelms one until one sees nothing but illness, trouble, and pain.

Self-pity is a concentration upon *nufs*, the cause of all disharmony. When one concentrates upon God, nothing but love will be found, but when the attention is centered around the thought of self, all ugliness, pain, and illness will rise. Of course in a certain sense they were always there, but this concentration gives them more life. Self-pity deprives the body and mind of the usual life which is naturally bestowed upon them by the Grace of God. It feeds the elementals who derive their potency from human excrescences, and these elementals in turn increase trouble. Concentration upon darkness does not increase the darkness, but it does impede the opportunity for light and health to reach the place of sickness.

January 30

The heart is not living until it has experienced pain.

The angel lives in the heart-sphere but does not know pain. There is a lack of strength in the love. This is something like the natural love of the infant. It is only when love is tested that love can show its strength. If it turns to hate or any emotion, that shows there was no life in it.

Sufis are able to experience pain in the heart without being drowned by it. The various spiritual practices are exercises to the heart-muscles and to the heart faculties. This endows the heart with life; that is to say, it enables the heart to partake of experiences and to shed the Divine Light upon them, showing the proper way through all intricacies of external existence.

JANUARY 31

The pleasures of life are blinding; it is love alone that clears
the rust from the heart, the mirror of the soul.

Pleasure is the effect upon *nufs* of the radiations from the mind-mesh, which through the falling current of breath form the emotions. But all these are of indirect light, which is subject to the elements and becomes controlled by them. To rise above the elements it is necessary to touch the heart-plane. This is a realm of pure light not contaminated by the karmic swirl below the mind-mesh. That is the metaphysical explanation, but the explanation to the heart is clear—when it loves, all the rust and dust are purged from its bosom. This is its blessing. Its life is its own blessing—heart is the medicine for heart.

FEBRUARY 1

The pain of love is the dynamite that breaks up the heart,
even if it be as hard as a rock.

The natural condition of the heart is to be soft, ever in a state of living expansion and contraction. When the breath is confined to the region of gross vibrations that are beneath the mind-mesh no finer vibrations can reach the heart, which slowly hardens like cooling rock. Then it ceases to be pliable and may be brittle like hardened rubber. Nevertheless, it is never entirely dead.

If the heart is called into action after it has lost its mobility, it will suffer pain even as a muscle long in disuse will suffer pain when it resumes activity. But the only energy that can touch the heart is love, and this often comes in a shock, surprise, or catastrophe. Be it ever so hard, there is always the possibility of the heart awakening, and sometimes people who have fallen very low will be shocked into great activity by a disaster. This would not be necessary if the person had lived a holy life.

The kindlier person sometimes suffers pain without this deeper experience, but he or she arrives much sooner at the state when the ordinary disturbances of life no longer cause hurt. The indifference of the sage, far from showing absence of heart activity, conceals greatness of heart and wisdom.

FEBRUARY 2

Our virtues are made by love, and our sins are caused by a lack of it.

As the Sufi Thoughts teach, there is one moral, there is one virtue, which is Love. Particular virtues arise from the qualities displayed by Love in everyday affairs. Thus arise courage, mercy, kindliness, compassion, adoration, friendship, fidelity, charity, kinship, and many other virtues. Yet all are aspects of Love.

As soon as the heart ceases to be active, so soon the mind gains control over will, and the Love-Life energy from the higher spheres no longer touches the personality. This brings about the reign of sin over one. This is the fall of humankind, true of Adam and true of all his descendants.

FEBRUARY 3

Love is the essence of all religion, mysticism, and philosophy.

What is religion? It is our relation to God. What is mysticism? It is our realization of God. What is philosophy? It is our consideration of God. But what connects us with God and God with us? It is the Love-Light-Life described as *Logos*. As soon as any speech, thought, or feeling connects us with God, some of this Universal Energy touches another or returns to God. This connecting nexus is the very elixir of Love.

FEBRUARY 4

The fire of devotion purifies the heart of the devotee,
and leads unto spiritual freedom.

Vibrations which reach the heart are of finer nature than those which touch the mind sphere. They cannot be conveyed on the breath ordinarily; however, through *Fikr*, *Zikr*, and *Darood*, as well as through certain practices of refining the breath, the Divine Thought enables the Cosmic Energy to pierce through the mind-mesh and return toward the source. This is the first resurrection. This is the beginning of the process of initiation.

It has been explained, when a person, in adoration or supplication, turns toward God, the feeling is of the nature of fire in that it rises. But also it gives strength and courage and faculty to the devotee. This puts back into the heart the life which naturally belongs there. The giving of this life to the heart is the restoration of it to its normal condition which is nothing but freedom. Real freedom of the will does not consist of catering to every desire. Freedom of the will consists of freeing it from all the excrescences of conditioned existence (*Samsara*) so its actions will not be hampered. This is only attained on the heart plane.

FEBRUARY 5

Mysticism without devotion is like uncooked food;
it can never be assimilated.

Mysticism means recognition of God. But how can one recognize God until the heart is awakened? It is only when, through the fire of devotion and love, the whole life force is returned to its source in fervor and contemplation that the spiritual life can be experienced.

FEBRUARY 6

One who stores evil in one's heart cannot see beauty.

Evil, being of the nature of shadow or darkness, destroys spiritual vision, and so blinds one to the beauty which was the purpose of creation. This condition should be called *avidya*, blindness or ignorance.

There is, however, a difference between one who has evil in the mind and evil in the heart. The average person who does not know or seek truth may be called evil in mind. This person is under the sway of sin, as the Christians explain and has been demonstrated. But there is another sort of person called diabolical, who may be mentally alert but who has deliberately turned the heart into a charnel house, a hidden chamber where evil is planned to be committed in the world. These people can put wicked thoughts into the minds of others and can command evil elementals to influence others so that they may never perform any particular vile act directly.

This shows that all evil thought, desire, or speech may be responsible for the wrong acts of others. In this there is universal Karma, which was the explanation of the Buddha. So long as anybody sows Karma, it prevents others from being delivered from pain, disease, injury, and death.

February 7

The wise, by studying nature, enter into unity through its variety,
and realize the personality of God by sacrificing their own.

It should not be supposed that Allah does not have a physical body. All nature, all the physical world, constitutes this body just as all the mental world constitutes the sheath of Allah's Mind. We cannot so easily see the inside of our body and cognize the various activities going on in the organs and cells, in the nerves and blood stream. In some mysterious way these constitute a unity, but such unity is fundamental to their existence.

Similarly, all the functions and species of nature are dependent upon a cosmic unity, which is reflected in them and is causal to them, but which does not consist of them. To understand this more fully, one must find out God's Mind in order to understand God's Body. This can only be done when one's own mind, and so one's own personality, is left behind in one's spiritual unfoldment.

February 8

Love manifests towards those whom we like as love;
towards those whom we do not like as forgiveness.

The love we feel toward friends and relatives and heroes is natural. Although Christ said, "Love ye your enemies," this does not mean to entertain the identical feeling toward them. Why? Because feeling is that which connects parties and unites them. We are united to our dear ones by love. By whatever the feeling we hold to those we do not like, they may not feel friendly toward us.

The proper attitude is therefore selflessness, to refuse to hold the feeling of dislike. The enemy, not appreciating our love, could not see it as love or friendship but could perceive it in the spirit of forgiveness. From our point of view it would be the same in both cases, but the object of love and the connection between ourselves and the other would be different in each instance.

FEBRUARY 9

Love brought humankind from the world of unity to that of variety, and the same force can take us back again to the world of unity from the world of variety.

First came God, and then the object of God's Love, which is called Creation. Then God in Love entered into union with this Creation and all the living forms appeared, the highest being humankind, which is the one resembling the Spiritual Parent most. But God, not being human, loves and can enter into union with all creatures as soon as that creature—atom, rock, earth, stone, plant, vegetable, bird, beast, fish, crawling creature, human being, *jinn*, spirit, or angel—turns toward God. The difference between this second kind of union—where love takes us back again to unity from variety—and the first—where we are brought by love from unity to variety—is that in the second instance one becomes entirely united with God, without necessarily producing any further fruits of union.

FEBRUARY 10

Whoever knows the mystery of vibrations indeed knows all things.

As aspiration this may appear to be a nice saying, or we may appreciate it intuitively as truth. The first stage is one of appreciation. That is only subjective; it has no objective vitality. One has no knowledge; one does not know it to be true although one may firmly believe it. Nevertheless, if it were said to such a one, "Whoever knows the mystery of vibrations does not know it or through it know God," how would you disprove such a statement?

Suppose it were said, "God is above vibration, above all vibrations, and so long as we deal with vibrations we are not contacting reality." A little meditation on the above shows the need for greater growth and understanding. It would be evident that you could read a thousand aphorisms and have a billion beliefs and this would not bring you any nearer the truth, except that it might put you in a proper receptive mood.

Then how **is** one to learn the mystery of vibrations? Mostly it happens through the breath, by watching the breath, but also by watching the heart and learning through the heart's awakening. As this is a practice and not a study, a deeper explanation without application would not help much.

FEBRUARY 11

One who arrives at the state of indifference without experiencing interest in life is incomplete and apt to be tempted by interest at any moment; but one who arrives at the state of indifference by going through interest really attains the blessed state.

This is very important. Sages all extol the value of indifference, but this indifference comes with an awakened heart. Many people are indifferent in the sense of being callous. Nothing moves them; they are like sticks or stones. That is not the real indifference. That is sloth, and it shows that the soul is asleep, there is no love, and there is no God-vitality.

Now the sages are very different, who know through their own experience the value and the lack of value in attachment in friendship, emotion, and in all of the vicissitudes of life. They surrender all forms of clinging. They no longer cling to anything, and they make an actual surrender. That shows the Divine Indifference.

FEBRUARY 12

Wisdom is greater and more difficult to attain than intellect, piety, or spirituality.

Intellect and piety are both connected with the mind and show attachment to name and form. Spirituality is a higher state which shows the heart awakening, but not necessarily awakened. Wisdom is the fruit of spirituality, when the heart condition is sustained, and the Divine Love-Life-Light is expressed and divulged through the personality.

FEBRUARY 13

Wisdom is intelligence in its pure essence, which is not necessarily dependent upon the knowledge of names and forms.

This intelligence is the natural faculty and condition of the heart when it is not veiled by the mind, when the activity of the consciousness is focused in the depths of one's being. Wisdom may be considered as the apperception or grasping of the fundamental principles which lie beneath name and form. While these principles can be perceived through particulars and do operate through particular forms, atoms, and vibrations, they are essentially aspects of *Nuri Mohammed*, that is to say, of the Divine Mirror of God into which Mohammed gazed. When one gazes into that mirror, this knowledge, called by the Sufis *Ilm*, is identical with Wisdom, God-knowledge, or *Tasawwuf*.

FEBRUARY 14

One forms one's future by one's actions; one's every good or bad action spreads its vibrations and becomes known throughout the universe.

The physical and mental creation may be considered as one personality. Humankind forms the Grand Human Being, sometimes known as Adam. This includes all the Life beneath the mind-mesh. The world above the mind-mesh, called by the Sufis *Djabrut*, is identical with Eden. Adam expelled from Eden is the picture of all of humanity functioning in the worlds of limitation. Whatever any personality does affects this whole kingdom of humanity as well as oneself.

Of course each one's actions affect oneself most of all. One's every word, speech, and thought strike the dome of *Malakut* and fall back again to their natural place. This return of energy not only touches the individual but touches the whole of humanity. It is like when a person spreads germs or disease, everyone might be liable. This shows the inclusive nature of Karma. In the same way kindness spreads abroad and the tales of good deeds often bear fruit in faraway places.

FEBRUARY 15

The universe is like a dome; it vibrates to that which you say in it, and answers the same back to you; so also is the law of action; we reap what we sow.

Human beings were placed in an enclosure where we were given full command over everything within. This is in the story of Adam. But to regain Eden we have to work out our destiny. For this purpose we were given the faculty of knowledge of name and form. Having this faculty we are responsible for our use or misuse of it.

But within certain limits there is the law of the equality of action and reaction. This means that if we suffer without doing evil, in time this will lead to compensation; while if we seem to escape punishment, we are only preparing a greater blow for ourselves. The effect of Karma is escaped by speaking, thinking, and acting in the name of God. Through the spiritual practices, we rise to wisdom above knowledge and suffering.

February 16

We are always searching for God afar off,
when all the while God is nearer to us than our own soul.

Differences in planes are not differences in time and space but differences of rates of vibrations. One plane is formed from another in the same region, called *akasha* or accommodation, by change of rate of vibration. Consequently all planes may be regarded as all spaces. God, being the source of formation and the essence of energy, is therefore in all times and all spaces and places and can be found by a change in pitch, by a tuning of the soul.

So long as soul is regarded as something different than material, something different from mental existence, one finds differences not soul. Since God is to be found in the mental and material, God is therefore the nearest thing. Really it is God Who is searching for God, and we are the very thing we are looking for, only in our ignorance we do not know this.

February 17

Concentration and contemplation are great things;
but no contemplation is greater than the life we have about us every day.

It is very easy to build dreams of ideals. It is very easy to imagine happiness in Heaven, but that brings no strength; it never brings that great satisfaction you feel when you have accomplished something. This satisfaction is greatest in the physical sphere where there is so much to overcome. This is the greatest battle it is possible to wage and its victory is the finest victory, the victory over great obstacles.

It is easy to imagine *Nirvana* far away from turmoil; it is marvelous to imagine and attain *Nirvana* in the midst of trouble. Therefore if the sage once finds the Universal Peace in the midst of strife, it will be natural to find it anywhere and everywhere. The descent of Jesus into Hell is nothing but the willingness of the awakened soul to face all and fear nothing for the sake of God.

FEBRUARY 18

One who expects to change the world will be disappointed;
one must change one's view. When this is done, then tolerance will come,
forgiveness will come, and there will be nothing one cannot bear.

Change of view does not mean simply to accept another person's view. Particular view is the standpoint of the *nufs*; accepting another's idea is to fall under the sway of *nufs*, in this case the *nufs* of another. The Sufi point of view is to perceive God's position, and when one can view life from the universal aspect as God sees it, it will include all points of view. This brings tolerance naturally, not as a moral, not as a discipline, but as the very part and portion of life. Then one will tolerate and forgive because one will not only see the other's viewpoint, one will know how and why the other came to that conclusion and will not separate the ideas from the whole life's experience of another. This is tolerance with wisdom and understanding.

FEBRUARY 19

To renounce what we cannot gain is not true renunciation; it is weakness.

We see this in the story of the fox that abandoned its quest for the grapes on the high branch that it couldn't reach. Those who call it "surrender" or "renunciation" when they cannot obtain an object sought make the prime error of assuming that they are that limited thought of self, called *nufs* by the Sufis, but this concept is not really the true Self. Whatever be the true cause of failure, it is due to lack of concentration and some weakness. Of course, very often ignorance leads us to believe that we might secure some unwarranted prize, which later knowledge shows is beyond our reach. In this case it was the weakness which was the cause of ignorance.

Spiritual renunciation is of a very different character, being surrender of that which we can easily obtain, or sacrifice of something which we possess and prize, or giving away something we have earned at great cost, or abandoning the fruits of action for some higher ideal. This is the true renunciation, the real spiritual sacrifice.

FEBRUARY 20

The religion of each one is the attainment of one's soul's desire;
when one is on the path of that attainment one is religious;
when one is off that path then one is irreligious, impious.

Religion in its highest and truest sense being that which relates us to God, it is the fulfillment of this relationship which alone satisfies the soul. This means the renunciation and abandonment of everything belonging to the three worlds of body, mind, and spirit. So long as we hold any earthly or heavenly attachments our love is not for the *Zat*, or absolute nature of God. When love is other than for the *Zat* of God, one may be called irreligious. One is impious in the sense that this failure to keep on the right path will lead one sooner or later to error and sin, and this keeps one bound by karmic ties.

FEBRUARY 21

The reformer comes to plough the ground;
the prophet comes to sow the seed; and the priest comes to reap the harvest.

In the physical world we find these stages. First someone comes to combat evil, often failing. Then another comes who moves human hearts and minds, and finally the third person becomes the leader in the righteous cause. On the mental plane we have the one who exhorts but does not move; this is the reformer; although some reformers are very successful in moving human emotions they do not always touch the mind or heart. The prophet is of another character. He or she places the seed of righteousness in the mind and heart that it may fructify. The movement that the prophet has founded becomes organized, often as a religion, and the priest is the leader in religion.

From another point of view, the reformer helps to clear away emotional rubbish, the prophet helps to keep the mind pure, and the priest helps to preserve the purity in the heart after it is once attained.

FEBRUARY 22

Life is an opportunity given to satisfy the hunger and thirst of the soul.

If the soul continued to exist only in the highest state, it would never experience hunger and thirst. These come through the separation, through its departure from its home, whence it passes through the phases of hunger and thirst. This is the theme of the opening of the **Masnavi**, the allegory of the flute. After the soul has suffered thoroughly in the pain of separation, it recovers step by step its lost province. As it throws off the deceiving desires, as it abandons the fruits of action, as it surrenders all the thoughts and attachments of incarnate and disincarnate experience, it comes again to the full satisfaction of love and the end of hunger and thirst in its reunion with God. This reunion, however, is only apparent; it has always existed, but the soul has not realized it during its journey away from home.

FEBRUARY 23

Truth alone can succeed; falsehood is a waste of time and loss of energy.

Truth metaphysically connotes all that is beyond the mental sphere, while falsehood is all that lives upon the shadow forms of the lower worlds. Truth is of the nature of Light and therefore of energy, while falsehood is of the nature of passing or incidental phenomena. The cause of falsehood is the *nufs*, that thought of self; where *nufs* does not exist there can be no falsehood. Therefore angels always tell the truth, but there is no merit in it. The successful person is one who, unlike the angels, has the ability to cling to falsehood and does not. Then one becomes master of all the energy and dominates the three worlds.

FEBRUARY 24

Do not fear God, but consciously regard God's pleasure and displeasure.

Fear is an emotion which results from the failure of breath to touch the heart plane. This is the natural human condition. In the opposite condition, that of love, the breath reaches but does not penetrate the heart-plane (*Djabrut*). However, the light of Intelligence confers upon human beings vision into that sphere so one can perceive the Divine Will. Thus one can, through the practice of *Darood* or *Fikr*, discover all that is in harmony or disharmony with God, and in a very practical (not theoretical) manner, perform God's Will.

February 25

One who has failed oneself has failed all;
one who has conquered oneself has won all.

Failure is due to the domination of the false self. It alone puts out the thought of failure, of weakness, of limitation. It is not capable of sustaining concentration or effort. When one has controlled this self and its passions, and especially when one has performed the spiritual practices which link one to God, the True Self, one has conquered this false lower self. This is the great victory of life. All other victories are unimportant in comparison with it and not essential to mundane existence. Once the *nufs* is mastered, the key to every success is at hand. This is conveyed in the allegory found in the original version of the movie, *The Thief of Baghdad*, starring Douglas Fairbanks, Senior.

February 26

As one rises above passion, so one begins to know what is love.

What is passion? What is love? They are the same force, in the former instance operating in the sphere of plurality, in the latter case in the world of unity or principle. When the Universal Love-Light is caught in the image of self, it is reflected in myriad pieces, each of which the self desires to grasp and keep as its own. Not recognizing the Supreme Unity and failing to find all its desire in any one of these fragments, the false self flits from false love to false love. This is because it only recognizes falsehood and not truth. Passion is therefore the shadow of love; it is not to be condemned. It is the selfishness which must be eradicated.

FEBRUARY 27

Believe in God with childlike faith; for simplicity with intelligence
is the sign of the Holy Ones.

Complexity is human born; humankind loves complexities. This is due to the activity of the mind-mesh which splits truth into fragments, the shadows of which appear as facts. Not all the facts combined will present the truth, nor can all facts be combined until the essence of truth is discernible.

It is the perception of unity, very simple in itself, very intelligible, yet quite unanalyzable, which is the natural aspect of the heart, characteristic of children and angels and possible in all souls who have escaped the network of the mind-mesh.

FEBRUARY 28

One who can live up to one's ideal is the ruler of life;
one who cannot live up to it is life's slave.

It is better to be obedient to a simple standard than to strive for some unattainable goal. Success does not depend upon the goal; success depends upon our overcoming obstacles. Many think that if they claim some noble ideal or moral standard they are fulfilling duty in life. This is a human conclusion. Success comes from mastering our own weaknesses, and if we do not coordinate the efforts of thought, speech, and deed, we cannot accomplish much. It is the unity of our self with our self that brings us sooner or later to full realization of unity.

FEBRUARY 29

Every moment of our life is an invaluable opportunity.

Every breath brings with it something from heaven; every breath takes with it something to heaven. There are the thoughts we get and the thoughts we give, there are the words we get and the words we give, there are the things we get and the things we give. All this is part of life, but there is more: according to our union with God every moment of our lives is permanent success obtained or lost.

MARCH 1

Nature speaks louder than the call from the minaret.

The call from the minaret is the call of human to human in the name of God, but in nature we find the call of God to the human in the Name of God, which is really the call of God to God in the Name of God. It is through the speech or call of God that the universe was made, and one reason that it was created was so that God could use it as the Divine Instrument for Eternal Music. That our ears are closed is not God's fault.

Yet we sense this call in another way, in our appreciation of sunshine, the song of birds, the falling waters, the dashing waves, the feeling of exuberance at springtime, the refreshing atmosphere after a rain, and in many other ways. Truly the Music of God is everywhere, but our artificial life has benumbed our ears. So someone must call us to prayer and worship, prayer and worship which are the natural business of the soul.

MARCH 2

*The priest gives a benediction from the church;
the branches of the tree give blessing from God.*

What is the church? It is not wrong to go to church or worship in church. Church is right where it unites men and women in prayer and worship and so promotes unity and kinship; it is wrong when it excommunicates or antagonizes men and women and so divides humanity. Such division is human, not divine. God does not condemn on any human basis; God is not bound by any decisions of human councils or human institutions.

Priest speaking in the name of self or in the name of church with thought of self cannot give the divine blessing. Tree, having no thought of self, rapt in love for God, can give the highest blessing and many people, believers and unbelievers alike, feel it.

MARCH 3

The soul brings its light from heaven; the mind acquires its knowledge from earth. Therefore, when the soul believes readily, the mind may still doubt.

The soul is always in light, can never be in anything but light because the soul is light. Mind makes accommodation for both light and darkness—light from heaven, darkness from earth. When mind draws its content from earth and picks up shadow-thoughts and shadow-words, instead of the light-substance embodied in those thoughts and words, it cannot have surety. For not only is shadow not light, but the tendency of shadow is to change its shape, to become smaller or larger, dimmer or deeper as light approaches or recedes. Under such circumstances the mind can never be too sure of this earth-born intellectual mind-gathering called "knowledge," which is nothing but the collection of names and forms and not true knowledge.

MARCH 4

Those who throw dust at the sun, the dust falls in their eyes.

This is literally true, but there is a much deeper significance. When someone offered injury to Buddha, he refused to accept the injury, classifying it as a gift, which whether acceptable or unacceptable, when refused was returned to the giver. The same idea is in Christ's, "Resist not evil." When one refuses to accept evil as evil, declining to recognize anything as harmful to the self, the intended harm or evil falls back upon the schemer.

The same law can be observed in the life of the great Sufi Bayazid Bistami. When he declared the universality of God in such a way as to betray the Great Secret, he called upon his disciples to kill him; but instead, their knives were turned back upon themselves. In other words, when we rise above duality, when we touch infinity, we can no longer be affected by the finite. And the one who wishes to do good to the sages receives good, while the one who desires to perform evil, receives evil. In that condition where he or she has risen above duality the sage is the master of Karma, above the influence of Karma.

MARCH 5

One creates one's own disharmony.

This occurs through one's thought of self, the *nufs*. Undifferentiated Sound exists above the mind-mesh, and in the mental plane it exists as all different sounds. These need not clash but when they are attuned to particular ears, and then focused by particular thoughts—especially by that *nufs*, or thought of self—their real rhythm and vibration is affected and they are perceived as disharmonies. Such disharmony is not real, it is not objective, it is subjective—the result of relating reality to the false self.

MARCH 6

The real abode of God is in the human heart; when it is frozen with bitterness or hatred, the doors of the shrine are closed, the light is hidden.

The effect of this freezing of the heart can be perceived in three ways. Physically it interferes with the free passage of blood through the veins and tubes and so produces various diseases—arthritis, rheumatism, angina, and all forms of sluggishness. Mentally it inhibits the passage of thought vibrations into the nerves, tends to sarcasm and bitterness in speech, and gross selfishness in outlooks upon life. Spiritually it kills all desire for love, growth, and expansion. The person recognizes no love or kindness either in his or her self or that of another, and without necessarily giving way to hate, leaves no room for the expression of spirit. So this man or woman stands in his or her own light, and there is a tightening up of all tendencies and functions—bringing decay and death, due to the absences of life. Even cancer and other such diseases can destroy the body because there is no room for the higher aspects of life and no protection against evil influences from within or without.

MARCH 7

It is a false love that does not uproot one's claim of "I";
the first and last lesson of love is "I am not."

There is difficulty of expression for love is above all expression. The nature of love is light, expansiveness, brightness, beauty, life itself. Thoughts, words, descriptions of any kind, arising from activity below the mind-mesh, can in no way describe the illimitable. The thought of self, any expression of selfhood, arises from name and form which are the shadows of reality. These names and forms can only be expressed by the marks they make, and their essence remains hidden. True love expresses itself in life, in atmosphere, in feeling, in heart qualities, in unselfishness; these are its characteristics which are removed from both affirmation and negation. It is life that lives, and love is life itself.

MARCH 8

You cannot be both horse and rider at the same time.

You are either the positive pole or the negative pole, the teacher or the pupil, *jelal* or *jemal*, leader or follower. In another aspect, horse represents mind and rider will; either the mind overshadows will or will directs and controls mind. There are no alternatives. But when one keeps in *Darood* and in unity with God, the part that one may play in the world does not matter. One may assume a seeming negativity, but one's full, honest, and real negativity is only toward God and God's Messengers. Toward all the rest of the world, inwardly one keeps a positive atmosphere and attitude when one knows and a negative (or receptive) one when one does not know.

MARCH 9

It is more important to know the truth about one's self
than to try to find out the truth of heaven and hell.

Heaven and hell are themselves the results of deeds. In the Bible the form of earth was conceived before sun and moon. Sun and moon represent higher and lower aspects of heaven, and the dark of the moon corresponds to hell. In finding the Self, the true Self which is God, we rise above both heaven and self.

From another point of view, considered metaphysically, the reality of existence is above the mind-mesh, is beyond *Malakut*, and heaven and hell are phases of the life in *Malakut*. Until we get beyond *Malakut* we do not touch the world of Principle.

MARCH 10

Everyone's pursuit is according to their evolution.

This means pursuit of pleasure, pursuit of wealth, pursuit of knowledge, pursuit of God, pursuit of love. What is the basis of pursuit? It is that the soul has an unsatisfied longing. No matter what the path in life, where there is pursuit it shows the soul has an unsatisfied longing. The sage knows the direction the pursuit should take, the average person does not; so the sage comes to satisfaction and finds peace of mind, heart, and soul, which are unrealized in the natures of the generality.

MARCH 11

We see what we see; beyond it we cannot see.

The vision of humankind as humankind is confined to the mind-mesh, but it is also true that God made the human being in God's own Image. By human being is meant what the Hebrews called *Aish*, the Intellectual Person. But this in turn was an aspect of Adam, the Universal Person, Whose vision extends beyond the mental plane.

The potentiality of humankind is greater than that of any domain in all the aspects of creation or existence. Our physical eye is like that of the animals, limited in scope, better than the eyes of some, not so good as the sight of others. But human eyesight is more closely connected with the human brain and mental life, and our mental eye is not like that of the animals. Some animals may see the sun and moon and be affected by them, but they never think about them, they do not compare their distances or size with the sizes and distances of objects about them. Indeed the mind of animals is totally different from that of the human being in certain aspects, particularly in the higher aspects. Imagination enables us to transcend time while animals are completely subject to time processes.

But the eye of our heart possesses capacity above limitation. This capacity, while it need not be called infinite, still is beyond the scope of mental vision and measurement. In that respect it is neither infinite nor finite nor quantitative nor qualitative; it is not subject to time or space, and is of a very different nature from time and space. So while Heart expands and contracts, opens and closes, it is therefore not of any geometrical or mathematical nature.

MARCH 12

The source of truth is within us; we ourselves are the object of our realization.

It is the discriminating faculty of the human mind that makes life so interesting, causes all this diversity and diversion yet at the same time makes for every sort of difficulty. The highest vibrations and the lowest are as one in principle, but through the analytical faculty of intellect they appear different and thus this faculty makes it difficult or impossible for one to realize unity. It is the realization of Oneness that takes a person above all discrimination and distinction. When this is accomplished you at once realize your unity in essence with all things, and with all thingness. But this also takes one above the realm of words and thoughts; these distinguish and define and are not of the nature of absolute unity.

MARCH 13

As life unfolds itself to one, the first lesson one learns is humility.

This living unfoldment is a process, not an accomplishment. It does not come from book learning or prayer or asceticism or from change in regimen or vain breathing exercises. It comes only through the grasping of life. And how is life grasped? It is either through actual pain and suffering, or worldly experience, or inner awakening through the Grace of God, as in meditation and *Zikr*.

MARCH 14

God is truth, and truth is God.

There are just two ways to discuss this matter, the very nature and essence of which is really beyond discussion. From one point of view, the process of apprehension of truth is in the first place a living heart awakening and growth. Even then the reality of completion comes only after the heart is fully awakened, and the self explored. Word, form, thought, symbolism, effect, or explanation can but point to a sort of *Neti* ("not this"), as the Hindus describe it. That is to say, truth is depicted as being a reality that is different from anything and everything which can be depicted.

But from the metaphysical point of view, theosophically expressed, Truth, in the state and stage of Absolute Unity, is all which is called *Rupa* and *Arupa*—all that is in name and form and all that is without name and form, a Unity which while being Unity includes every degree and variety of complexity. So it is not only the life above the mind-mesh, it is the realization that this life beyond the mental, called Buddhic, includes also every sort of condition, actual and potential, so that all Heaven and Hell appear as part of one's being. This cannot be easily discussed, as it is clouded by every process except the highest forms of meditation and contemplation.

MARCH 15

Until one loses oneself in the vision of God, one cannot be said to live really.

That is to say, the limited life is not life. Mortality, which says life and death are two, not one, is not life. From one point of view, we die not only daily but with every breath. Attachment is birth and freedom from attachment is death. Therefore one must become free from every sort of attachment or clinging. One must become **free**.

And how does one become free? It is through apprehension of God which comes through God's Grace given to those who lose themselves in God. God's Grace is everywhere but we shut it out by our attachment. Detachment brings Grace and Grace brings detachment; they are one, not two.

Baqa, or awakening to the real self, is not something phenomenal or super-phenomenal. It is living with open eyes, with open consciousness, with understanding. It belongs neither to time nor space nor relativity. Until it is actually experienced, all consideration of it is vain. By shutting out self, one discovers it automatically.

MARCH 16

At every step of evolution, one's realization of God changes.

For the nature of mind is to seek, to move, to change. It may endeavor to enlarge its scope, and this brings change in realization. But *Baqa* is most wonderful for it includes both the changing and changeless condition at the same time. It brings the celestial music which is one note and all notes. Even discovery of God does not confer divinity. This is never possible in our sense of the term even though we may speak of *Parinirvana*. For the mind to dwell on such matters is senseless; for the mind to discover itself is all value.

MARCH 17

Verily, one is victorious who has conquered oneself.

What is the nature of victory? When one gains something from another, unless in that process one has gained strength, one has gained nothing. The things that one momentarily seizes one cannot keep when one leaves this world; the strength that comes to one either on the battlefield or in controversy or in love or in friendliness or in any situation—if it is really strength—can be taken with one out of this world. This shows that strength is something that can be gained, and a victorious person can gain strength.

Now suppose one is an athlete. It has been found by people we regard as ordinary that well-trained athletes, be they ball players or runners or wrestlers or pugilists, must keep a fairly strict regimen especially in regard to rhythm and self-control. No matter how great their physical prowess, without this rhythm and self-control they cannot consistently and continually win. Their whole life, be it ever so mundane and material, depends upon their self-control.

From this we can see that the nature of deliverance is not apart from the finite existence, that *Nirvana* and *Samsara* are of the same essence. And what is the sage? The sage is nothing but that athlete, that pugilist, who has carried that regimen over into the mental sphere from the physical. And what is the saint? He or she is one who has gone still further and carried this discipline into the heart, in other words into the whole of life.

MARCH 18

Prayer is the greatest virtue, the only way of being free from all sin.

What is this prayer? This prayer is the continual process of approach to God and submission to God's Will. If one prays a little, the prayer may be answered, but in the flux of things the answer may not be noticed and then one will doubt the merit of prayer. Mohammed instituted five prayers daily, which really meant a rhythmical concentration on God, and it was the sincere prayers in the mosque which brought victory to the armies on the battlefields. With the advent of insincerity came the dawn of defeat.

To the Sufis, cessation of prayer constitutes defeat. Every breath, every step, and every thought is a prayer for them. This is the great merit of *Fikr*, continually carrying the thought of God on the breath, so great it cannot be compared to anything else. By prayer, Sufis mean *Fikr*; God alone is wise, God alone is good, and therefore full dependence on God is the only and the greatest virtue.

MARCH 19

It is the sincere devotee who knows best how
to humble himself or herself before God.

Sincerity is spiritual humility. No one can say, "I am humble," for any expression "I am" precludes humility. Humility says, "Thou art," and it does not qualify or posit anything. It loses itself by itself.

MARCH 20

It is wise to see all things,
and yet to turn our eyes from all that should be overlooked.

It is the soul which sees, the heart which understands. Mind of itself is nothing, but mind properly trained and controlled gains the whole world without losing one's soul. In this condition one sees because God sees through one; one does not have to see for the sake of sight or for the sake of self, but for the sake of God one has to see. Now if we reflect upon what we have seen, if we give much thought to what we have seen, this is sight for the sake of self; it is not sight for the sake of God and our saying so does not make it so.

That sight which is Insight (*Kashf*) sees the attributes and essence together and has no need to analyze persons or situations. It sees the complete unity with all its parts, and yet does not attribute moral valuation to any condition or thing. This is having Right Views, where the fruits of sensation are left to God.

MARCH 21

Our soul is blessed with the impression of the glory of God
whenever our lips praise God.

This praise is the one thing which surely pierces the mind-mesh. In the first place, the praise we give to God is the one praise for which we cannot possibly expect return; this lack of expectancy of return shows unselfishness, and unselfishness is the one thing that blesses the soul.

MARCH 22

There is one teacher, God; we are all God's pupils.

Knowledge is not the fruit of the mind; knowledge comes when mind itself is the fruit of the tree of knowledge. It is not particular names and forms that constitute knowledge; it is the successful grasping of affairs through the living intelligence, which is the very essence of our self.

And what is this intelligence? It is the Spirit of Guidance within us, that is to say the reflection of God which is the one thing that gives us strength and inspiration. Beyond even that is God in Essence Who is continually pouring forth love and knowledge. When we are receptive we become God's disciples.

MARCH 23

All earthly knowledge is as a cloud covering the sun.

This is so because these forms arise from thought-shadows. It is the hardening of thought-forms which enables humankind to produce material objects out of the stuff of the physical sphere. The mental and physical cannot be dissociated in this, but the process that enables the mind to work is super-mental. Real knowledge comes when mind is tuned to heart and heart to that universality which we call God or Allah or Amitabha or Brahma.

MARCH 24

The first sign of the realization of truth is tolerance.

Truth being of the Buddhic nature, not *manasic* (mental), it can never be properly expressed in words. You cannot build a syllogism about Love, neither can you describe Truth. Even the attempt to describe Truth is wrong in itself. All attempts are wrong because they are attempts, and yet all attempts are right because they are concentrations upon what is right and thus are of the nature of right concentration.

From this point of view, it can be seen that all endeavor is good, but all expression is imperfect. The difference between right and wrong being relative and not absolute, and there being none of whom it can be said that they are always right, the spiritual tolerance comes from seeing that all expressions are part right and part wrong and that their source of error is in their being expressed and not in what is actually expressed.

This is very different from the tolerance practiced by mentalists who nevertheless feel their own view is right. It shows greatness of heart in being fair-minded toward those who differ. But the spiritual person knows that it is of the very nature of *nufs*, or ego-self, to differ, and that all yearning for truth is wrong, and that all expression of truth is nothing but this *nufs*, albeit there are several degrees or aspects of *nufs*.

MARCH 25

One who is filled with the knowledge of names and forms has no capacity for the knowledge of God.

Yet one who has found capacity for the knowledge of God has all capacity for knowledge of names and forms. That is because the heart is so much greater than the mind and is the very essence of mind. Growth of heart, awakening of heart, purifying of true faith—these are the best means of increasing the capacity of mind. However, the object of life is the attainment of truth, not the development of mind. Sufis often have acquired great intellects through their spiritual unfoldment, but it is not necessary, it has no merit because this knowledge as such cannot be taken above *Malakut*.

Suppose one is living the life of the heart, whether in *Djabrut* or on earth—and it is really the same thing—how does such a one acquire knowledge? One does not need it at all. One can read it in the minds of others, not only in the human mind, but when the heart is open, the very trees, hills, flowers, rocks and birds and animals will convey their impressions to one, and there is a silent speech which is vastly larger than any sounds made by the tongue.

Besides that, in the heart condition there is no need to entangle the mind or carry a large memory. It is always there in the atoms and can be picked up at will. This is the higher *akasha* that holds all the knowledge of existence and forms, so to speak, the *prakrit* or physical manifestation of *Djabrut*, the Adamic, which becomes the sky of *Malakut* from another point of view.

MARCH 26

We are closer to God than the fishes are to the ocean.

Now the fishes are in the ocean but the ocean is not in the fish except in a certain sense. The fish have bones, muscles, etc., which are of more solid materials than the ocean. But all things are of God, the material of which the human being is formed, the *akasha* which provides the substance and food for the intellect, the stream of light which is the essence of heart, and the soul which is God.

MARCH 27

We start our lives trying to be teachers; it is very hard to learn to be a pupil.

Because being a pupil is not a kind of learning, it is a surrender. Until self is surrendered one cannot learn from another. So long as one holds on to self, the door is shut before all other selves, whether it is the *nufs* of a human, animal, plant, rock, thought of anything in the heavens above or in the earth below. All this is shut out beyond a certain point.

When this *nufs* is restrained, all vibrations convey to the heart all that the heart needs. This is the beginning of being a pupil, yet after years of meditation and prayer, one does not always attain to the heart condition or sustain it. At the same time, pain or love or sorrow can bring it all in an instant.

MARCH 28

Until the heart is empty, it cannot receive the knowledge of God.

Now the true condition of the heart is this, that it carries nothing. It cannot contain two things, but the unity it holds in love may be simple or complex, very large or greater than the whole universe. This is the explanation of the teaching of the Upanishads. In the Upanishads, *Atman* often means the same as heart-essence, and this heart-essence grasps both great and small, but whatever it holds, it holds nothing else.

For that reason Sufis practice heart-concentration, first to restore to the heart its faculty of grasping and then to prepare the heart for grasping that which alone does it good; that is to say, to grasp God, to hold God. All Sufi practices have this object in view.

MARCH 29

According to one's evolution, one knows truth.

That is to say, to the degree that one's heart opens one knows truth. Until this occurs, there may be knowledge of names and forms—this is not Truth. Until this occurs, one may be kind to everybody and have friends or disciples or happiness, but this is not Truth. All these are passing fancies whether of the seeming essence of knowledge or love. Until the mind-mesh is pierced and reality perceived, it is not Truth. Truth is above all worldly knowledge and morality. It is we ourselves who are of the nature of Truth, and not anything outside can be called Truth.

MARCH 30

We can never sufficiently humble our limited self before limitless perfection.

So long as there is humility, effacement is not yet reached. Through humility we make very little of our limited self; through effacement we make it as nothing. The small fraction has a value, it may be a very little value, but it still has some value; so humility keeps the ego from expanding itself but does not efface it.

Now in mathematics all numbers are as nothing before the Infinite, and in reality all things or thoughts are as nothing before God. This corresponds to humility. But in mathematics the zero is as nothing before anything which has any value, without taking measure of the thing. This is the effacement of ego, where all things appear as Infinite because in everything one sees God's Face.

MARCH 31

Even to utter the name of God is a blessing that can fill the soul
with light, joy, and happiness as nothing else can do.

While this may be true, while there may be a great mantric value in repetition in thought and speech of any name for God, the merit is nothing compared to the reality one experiences as in *Zikr* when one completely dissolves in the remembrance of Unity. That is to say, this remembrance is not a karmic activity; it is not the piling up of some good for which one may receive a future reward, whether in or out of heaven. In *Zikr* this blessing is actually what happens; therefore it is not so important to discuss why it happens but to know that it happens. The great understanding comes from and through the living experience. Praising God is its own reward.

APRIL 1

When one praises the beauty of God, one's soul is filled with bliss.

Now the condition of soul is peace, but in its natural, active state soul operates in the sphere of heart where the condition is bliss. That is to say, the soul praises God. This praising God brings bliss and this state of bliss is not connected with any plane. It is our state of mind which determines the plane, not the condition of soul, which is above conditioned existence. At the same time, whenever the mind permits the praising of God in or out of prayer, it raises the whole pitch of the personality and purifies the breath in the highest manner. This leads to bliss.

APRIL 2

Sympathy is the root of religion, and so long as the spirit of sympathy is living in your heart, you have the light of religion.

Religion is that which connects one with God. Therefore it is not mental, and not being mental there can be no theology or system of beliefs. When a mother suckles an infant there is no system of beliefs, there is not any intellectual enterprise. She loves it because she loves it, and this is very much simpler to explain than the love between God and the soul.

Now the feeling between mother and child, between God and soul which is called love, or *agape* by the Christians, *Ishk* by the Sufis and Muslims generally, *karuna* by the Buddhists and has other names elsewhere, is the great driving power in the Universe. This sympathy is the same force which appears as cohesion, adhesion, and gravitation among the physical forces; this promotes all growth—physical, mental, or spiritual—and is the principle behind many faculties which appear in the world of creation.

As its essence is super-mental; it can be appreciated without being completely understood by mind. Nor is this necessary. Everyone can express sympathy or feel it from another; all that is therefore necessary is to perceive that that feeling and not any system of beliefs, is the fundamental root of real religion.

APRIL 3

Life is a misery for the one absorbed in oneself.

The one who is absorbed in self makes a load of every experience by relating it to the ego. The world has moved and will move without this ego, and events will take place, and no personality is ever so powerful that, without divine help, he or she can cause the world to change its course.

We only feel pain when we think of self; we feel no pain when we think of God, especially when we praise God. Praise of God leads to bliss, and when there is bliss there is no pain. There is a spiritual anesthetic in praise which can cure all suffering. There is nobody who will appear harmonious before everyone. When one possesses the thoughts and feelings another has toward their person, one grasps these disharmonies, and these impressions cause all manner of disease within the mind and within the body. But one does not have to possess those feelings; one does not have to accept all those thought vibrations others are sending out. One may refuse to accept them, whereupon the karmic effect goes back upon the cause, whether for good or ill.

Spiritual travelers therefore endeavor to remove the ego, so that there can be no collation of such vibrations, and so no opportunity for disease or suffering of any kind.

APRIL 4

To give sympathy is sovereignty; to desire it from others is captivity.

Ishk Allah. Sympathy (*Ishk*) is God; there is no difference. When one gives out sympathy, one is expressing God; one has found God whether conscious of it or not. But when one desires it, one has not found it; the search is not complete.

This sympathy is the very root-force of the Universe and when one comes to the heart of it—which is found even within the human heart—all keys to all mysteries are found. There is no lost key to mysteries other than love and sympathy, and to look for anything mental or magical or evocative is lost effort. By removing the ego in love and sympathy, with love and sympathy, the Golden Key becomes one's possession.

April 5

God speaks to the ears of every heart, but it is not every heart that hears.

All vibrations, from the throne of God to the physical plane, bound and rebound through the Universe causing the music of the spheres. This is the Message of God, in that it can be regarded as the very Message which God is speaking eternally. The theme of this Message, if it can be said to have a theme, can be epitomized in the English words "love," "harmony," and "beauty." That is to say, the perfected principle of all that is embodied in these words is emanated in and through these cosmic vibrations.

We generally do not consider light as anything but physical light, yet the plant feels that physical light not only as light but as life and love also. This can be seen both in its vertical growth and its daily horizontal movement in following the sun through the heavens. When the human heart is opened, it finds the spiritual light is also life and love, and while the human mind has created three words and may even regard these three words as representing three thoughts, this is because of its discriminating faculty which has the tendency to divide and define.

When one lays aside this discriminating faculty and begins to feel, after a while one finds that behind every word and thought there is a spirit, and this spirit is really what the Sufis call the Spirit of Guidance. In other words, God is taking on a name or form or feeling so that even an individuated person can receive the spiritual Guidance. This process proves that God is all-loving, all-merciful, all-sympathetic, all-tender-hearted.

April 6

As one can see when the eyes are open,
so one can understand when the heart is open.

This opening of the heart is not physiological, but even in the physical body the heart is affected. When *rigor mortis* sets in at death, the blood does not flow, the cells are not fed; in other words, the heart is closed and does not show any love to the body. Heart must love body that body live; heart must love mind that mind live. When body and mind keep heart closed, it is body and mind that suffer.

Now the spiritual condition of the opening of heart comes when the will is no longer dominated by the body and mind. Then the will-power, which is in reality love-power, can properly express itself through the heart. When will-power is in the heart it is at home, and when it is at home it is most powerful and yet most natural.

Sympathy and love expand the heart, enable the blood to flow freely, enable the thought to function actively and clearly, and by removing the concept of self, there is nothing in the Universe which cannot be apprehended.

April 7

It is being dead to self that is the recognition of God.

This is so simple that its very simplicity has astounded those who have found God. We are always looking for complexities, but these come out of the self-thought. Light is simple, although from it very complex mixtures of colors have been made. Yet the essence of all these colors is light which is much more simple. To find light in the colors, one has to move from the complex to the simple.

This is not a mental process when one is considering human spiritual evolution. It is the living process which comes when one ceases to think in terms of "I." This does not extinguish thought, it purifies thought. Instead of the "I" trying to think thought, it is pure thought which thinks. And how does thought think?

On the physical plane there are natural movements of matter, which have led some to believe there is no cause, and that the natural forces control everything. There is an element of truth in this belief as every activity of matter may cause some other matter to move, as in the phenomenon of weather. There is an analogous condition in the mental world that every thought of anyone may affect many other thoughts and produce mental phenomena. At the same time, just as the physical sun, which embodies physical light, is the most important factor in the physical world, so the sun of intelligence, embodying pure thought, affects the mental world more than anything else.

There are all kinds of clouds in the mental world, but these are produced by the self in opposition to the sun of intelligence. So one cannot enter the higher heavens in bliss until these clouds are removed; yet this removal, this extinguishing of self, automatically brings one into the presence of God, regardless of time, space, plane, or condition.

APRIL 8

As the light of the sun helps the plant to grow,
so the divine Spirit helps the soul towards its perfection.

Light has three aspects which have formed the phenomenon of sun in the physical, mental, and spiritual worlds respectively. In the physical world, the sun promotes the growth of plants as well as of animals and humans. In the mental world, the sun helps to increase the intellectual power of animals and humans. In the spiritual world, the sun awakens the heart by the process of sympathy and attunement, a principle found operating in the radio and in general where there are the so-called sympathetic vibrations of any kind.

APRIL 9

Things are worthwhile when we seek them; only then do we know their value.

But the real value is in the search, not in the things. In the story of "Sir Launfal" by the poet Lowell, the cup of Christ was as a cup of pure running water. It was not magical, but the search and the suffering brought the awakening. Actually no thing has great spiritual value, but to cease to search—to be unwilling to attain, not to look or strive—all these prevent God from manifesting and prevent us from returning to God's Source.

APRIL 10

When one looks at the ocean, one can only see that part of it which comes within one's range of vision; so it is with the truth.

Nevertheless, it is possible to become one with the ocean through selfless concentration, and it is also possible to become as one with Truth by selfless concentration. That light which falls below the mind-mesh depends upon the personality's degree of awakening. To increase the light it is necessary to develop the personality, and for this there is a definite spiritual method, the chief point of which is the education of the heart, which is not so much an education but an increase in life's experience. The more one can imbibe of life itself, the more one can appreciate Truth, and when one reaches that stage when one feels at one with the whole stream of life, one is not far from the goal.

APRIL 11

It does not matter in what way one offers one's respect and reverence to the deity one worships; it matters only how sincere one is in one's offering.

This is true because respect and reverence are determined by the degree of sincerity and selflessness and not by an outer act. We see this in the story of the widow's mite. Christ said that she had given the most to God, and it was because she had given herself and not because of any mathematical proportion of tithe. So we find many manners of prayer and ceremonials of worship and all names and forms, but these are mostly for human convenience. For God's sake we need sincerity, that is to say, the prayer of the heart which is the real and full prayer.

APRIL 12

The ideal of God is a bridge connecting the limited life with the unlimited; whoever travels over this bridge passes safely from the limited to the unlimited life.

Most words indicate that which the mind has grasped of the finite portion of existence. But this finite portion is not reality; it is shadow or color, and depends upon our own condition, not upon the thing or condition or principle apprehended. Now mind, realizing that all did not come within its ken and finding that the greater portion of life is not intellectually understood, made use of the word **God** or of some similar word to describe the *Pleroma*—the All-Embracing, Living Fullness which is felt to be by the ignorant and known to be by the wise. This feeling of God, which is the greatest intuition, through faith helps one greatly toward its realization.

April 13

The one who wants to understand, will understand.

This is the condition of will leading the mind. The will, being the efflux of the soul, wants to unite with God. The thought wants to turn the will toward variety. This brings about the struggle between peace and unity on the one hand and intoxication and variety on the other. Understanding comes from the grasping of unity, which is possible when selfhood is laid aside and the faculty of discrimination is lulled into quiescence.

April 14

We are the picture of the reflection of our imagination;
we are as large or as small as we think ourselves.

So long as our thought is centered around our concept of a limited self, we are limited by the power of thought; when we rise to the fullness of life in the Cosmic Unity, finding that God Alone is and is the True Self, we are no longer limited. And what was it that limited us? It was nothing but our own thought. Just as thought can obtain all knowledge of matter, so can spirit gain all knowledge of thought, and so can God-attainment give all knowledge of spirit.

April 15

The great teachers of humanity become streams of love.

Considered historically, this is so because we do find millions of people paying homage to the Messengers of God, whatsoever be their names, whatsoever was the form of their Message. From a higher point of view, they have been recognized as the guides of humanity, no longer limited by their physical vehicles and so able to assist those devoted to them, assisting them toward fuller realization and a greater devotion for That One Who is above all limitation, name, and form. Finally, when one comes more into contact with them in the very fullness of spirit, one finds them to be these very streams of love.

APRIL 16

"God is Love"—three words which open up an unending realm for the thinker
who desires to probe the depths of the secret of life.

In this we have three ideas, two of which the mind can partially grasp, the other of which—although the mind names it—it grasps not at all. This is "God," who in the form called by the Sufis *Zat*, is beyond all predication, but in the aspects of Life and Love, there is predication about God.

Thus when one says, "is," that means that God and the Life are identical. Allah is essence, Allah is Eternal Being, and thus "God is." God is and no one else is; God is and nothing else is. Only God is and there is naught else. But what is God? What is the nature of Life? It is Love. If it were not Love, nothing would hold on to anything else—neither cell to cell in the physical, nor thought to thought in the mental, nor heart to heart in the spiritual. Without love nothing would adhere to anything else, there would be nothing to know. All would be chaos. And upon this much meditation is needed.

APRIL 17

It is the surface of the sea that makes waves and roaring breakers;
the depth is silent.

This surface is the physical condition, but between the physical and mental is a similar condition. Thus speech operates by waves moving through the ocean of air, and through these waves we are able to understand another in part. But there could have been no words and no language if there was not some agreement to accept these word-symbols as expressions of thought. Thus thought makes itself known by waves, whether as sound in the physical or as waves, which we can call telepathic, in the mental.

Yet both these types of waves arise from the faculty of discrimination. They tell what they tell, not through and in principles, but through and in differences. All these vibrations are disturbances of the media through which they move, and every disturbance of any kind reacts according to the karmic law. So all thought, as well as all speech and action, which is not divinely harmonious to begin with, is of the nature of war, disease, disharmony, and disruption.

APRIL 18

Our success or failure depends upon the harmony or disharmony of our individual will with the divine Will.

All thought, speech, and action not divine in its operation causes disturbance. Therefore restraint of thought, speech, and action appears necessary to produce calmness and peace for ourselves or for the universe. But this is the calmness of sleep, not of activity, and approaches death, not life, in its principle. The great quest is to find the calmness that is action, the peace that is expressive, the principle which is harmonious in all its operations.

This comes through our union with God, and this in turn is the natural result of spiritual practices, especially *Fikr*. This permits action, allows the life to touch the surface, and spiritualizes even the dense earth, for as soon as human will touches Divine Will, then that instant the Divine Will is expressed through the human being. And for this purpose humanity was made to appear on the earth.

APRIL 19

The wave realizes "I am the sea," and by falling into the sea prostrates itself before its God.

This is the *Nirvana* of the wave. Yet all vibrations have their *Nirvana* when they reunite with their source, and all that has name finds its *Nirvana* when it is reunited with its source—which can only properly be termed the Nameless, although humans have been pleased to call it God, Allah, Brahma, and given it other terms. This is good so long as the Reality is not confused with the concept of Reality.

APRIL 20

The secret of happiness is hidden under the cover of spiritual knowledge.

And what is spiritual knowledge? It is unity-knowledge, that is to say, the knowledge which understands principles above their divisions into aspects, qualities, and attributes. This knowledge is not apart from principles or realities, for it cannot be attained until one can become that which is being apprehended, becoming known. In other words, there is to be union between seeker and sought, and it is love alone which accomplishes this union. Therefore spiritual knowledge and love are one and the same thing, and that love which does not include knowledge and that knowledge which does not include love will never bring happiness because either is incomplete. So long as the soul is not completely satisfied, there can be no abiding happiness.

APRIL 21

The soul is first born into the false self, it is blind;
in the true self the soul opens its eyes.

This is because in going toward incarnation, the soul was made drunk and becomes enticed by the wonders of the worlds of limitations. Then it becomes identified in its dream with that which it is dreaming and does not know it is false until it has awakened. Every spiritual practice enhances this awakening, which becomes fact when it sees that the false ego is the product of thought and not the originator.

APRIL 22

To learn the lesson of how to live is more important
than any psychic or occult knowledge.

Transcendental knowledge which is confined to the universe of limitation is subject to limitation. The knowledge of the psychic realm may take one beyond earth, but it does not take one to God. The knowledge of the mental and psychic and physical may seem to be without limit, yet it is nothing compared to the knowledge which transcends these spheres. Even all the heart can give as heart alone, separated from the pure stream of life, even that, which appears unlimited to the intellectual, even that is nothing to the comprehension of life itself which comes through self-sacrifice, through union with the source of all things and thoughts.

APRIL 23

Knowledge without love is lifeless.

This lifeless knowledge is the knowledge of the lower worlds, which is subject to death. For every time we forget, that is the death of this false knowledge, and every time we become indifferent, some of this ego-coined knowledge loses its false, elemental life. When one masters these elemental thoughts, when one realizes that principles can be understood only by union with these principles and that union connotes nothing but love, then one sees the real relation between head and heart, and the real process of the highest learning and the highest wisdom.

APRIL 24

The aim of the mystic is to keep near to the idea of unity,
and to find out where we unite.

In fact the aim of the Mystic is to keep always near to the idea of Unity, and this is possible by concentrating always on "Toward the One," which practice when carried on the breath is called *Darood.* This is the very gate to love and unity. By continuing in this state one finally feels the thoughts harmonizing with the self in an indescribable manner. Then the intuitions take one into life more, and trust in these intuitions takes one even further. Every time the breath appears out of harmony, there is weakness, and when it flows harmoniously, there is strength. This is the sign of life itself.

And where is this union? It is in the heart stream. It is the love-life which is beyond the mental sphere. The more the heart-life, the more the love-life, the more the acquisition of unity.

APRIL 25

Sleep is comfortable, but awakening is interesting.

This is true for the body. It is also true for the mind, which becomes tired, but even when we go to bed it sometimes is enticed by its thoughts. It is also true for the heart, which finds its peace and joy in loving one—be it person or God—yet keeps up so many interests that it may lose faith. Loss of faith is often accompanied by a humanitarian solicitude, but this solicitude, although well-meaning, is not founded upon principle and so may degenerate into sentimentalism.

Finally the soul itself sleeps and awakens, but its true condition is where these are united. In this world, the soul is as asleep except for momentary flashes. In the inner life, these flashes increase and finally there is the awakening. But this continual sleeping and awakening, states of contraction and expansion, or nearness and farness, belong to those on the path to God, not to the travelers who have arrived.

APRIL 26

Every moment has its special message.

Because there are thoughts we can grasp or let go by, because the breath brings with it something from Heaven which we can take or leave, because the Spirit of Guidance is ever present in the heart. So the Sufi prays, "Draw us closer to Thee every moment of our life until in us be reflected Thy Grace, Thy Glory, Thy Wisdom, Thy Joy, and Thy Peace."

APRIL 27

To make God a reality is the real object of worship.

And how is this done? By ceasing to act, think, speak or even feel as a disjunctive personality. Acting unity, thinking unity, speaking unity, feeling unity, and recognizing unity as nothing but love is one part of making God a reality. And the other part consists in coming to the realization of the falseness of everything that emanates from the limited personality. These together bring one to the marvelous discovery. And what is the marvelous discovery? That there is nothing to be discovered, that the thing searching itself was the thing to be found.

APRIL 28

Every passion, every emotion has its effect upon the mind,
and every change of mind, however slight, has its effect upon the body.

Now passions and emotions come from two sources—the breath and the ego. The breath is as the mother, for when the breath is spiritualized there can be no emotion unless indifference be regarded as such. But according to the elements dominant in the breath and according to the state of thought or feeling, there are emotions. And without the thought of self, there would be no passions or emotions for all arise from the attempt of the *nufs* "to be something."

Every emotion has its seat in some organ of the body, and under their stress either the fluid of these organs is thrown into the blood or the blood enters the organs. So the natural rhythm is affected and the body suffers accordingly. But the mind also suffers, for every activity of any organ enervates the nerves, the mental magnetism is drawn in that direction, and so thought as a whole is affected and perhaps impeded.

Likewise every thought, by drawing more nervous energy and mental magnetism, by attracting more blood and by directing the will-power, naturally takes the forces away from other parts of the body and mind. Thus, in deep thinking, physical exercise may be impossible, while one engaged in athletic pursuits is generally unable to carry on simultaneously intellectual tasks.

APRIL 29

When souls meet each other, what truth can they exchange?
It is uttered in silence, yet always surely reaches its goal.

When souls meet, there can be no speech, for the presence of speech means that it is minds that are meeting. But the essence of all souls is one, and therefore the meeting of souls is the union of souls, which cannot be comprehended or explained. It is a process, whereupon plurality becomes unity, wherein there are neither distinctions nor differences, no "I-ness" and "thou-ness," and in general the overcoming of all conditions which make for plurality. When souls meet, there are no souls: there is God and God alone.

APRIL 30

All gains, whether material, spiritual, moral or mystical,
are in answer to one's own character.

For either they come through the operation of karmic law wherein one attracts or repels because of one's nature, or else they come because of the Grace of God which, although ever-present, is not accepted until the self is laid aside. This is the perfuming of character.

MAY 1

You can have all good things, wealth, friends, kindness, love to give,
and love to receive, once you have learned not to be blinded by them;
learned to escape from disappointment, and from repugnance
at the idea that things are not as you want them to be.

To begin with, the idea of "good things" must be altered; altered not to eliminate what we may call valuable, but rather augmented to include many things we may not call valuable. What we call valuable must have some value; otherwise it would not be prized. The pursuit of wealth is not wrong of itself but becomes wrong when it displaces higher ideals. The ideal pursuit is an all-inclusive pursuit which does not neglect the sustenance for body, heart, or soul.

So first we must include in the term wealth, not only material good, but intellectual gifts and the treasures of the spirit. But besides that, it is important to possess these things, and not to be possessed by them. So long as we pursue them, it is only to be possessed by them, but when in our search for the Highest we come into temporary possession of goods, then it cannot be said that we possess them, for then God possesses them.

So it is with friends. To possess friends we must understand the highest friendship, and this is only possible with the realization of God. Otherwise our so-called friends are as possessions, which we try to include in our thoughts of ownership until we become owned by these thoughts. And the same is true concerning kindness, the faculty by which and through which friends are attained and maintained. That kindness which is adopted as an affectation is false, and that which is the natural outburst of the heart is true.

And this right attitude in life becomes more than true when we consider love from any standpoint. It is impossible for us to love all unless the spiritual love of God is in our heart. We may use the word "love" and make claims, but there will be no life in it and it will fail when the test comes, for it will be centered around the *nufs*. Use of the word "love" is very different from the substance love.

Therefore the question arises whether we are blinded by our desires or ideals, or whether we control them. When we control them, nothing can either elate us or disappoint us. Both these are forms of intoxication—the former intoxication (of ideals) by light, the latter intoxication (of desires) by darkness—and perhaps the latter may sometimes be preferable to the former which is sometimes so blinding that one cannot easily recover the sight of heart and soul.

Finally we must consider the condition of things as the result of all thoughts of all beings. We cannot control the thoughts of others. We might influence them in part, but God has given will-power to all humankind. Through this thoughts are formed, and through these thoughts the material affairs of the world are fixed.

The consequence is tremendous, that not only is each individual but one part of billions of people, all of whose thoughts and whose Karma is affecting the world, but the influence of the past is still greater. Not only our reverence for people of the past, but constitutions, contracts, and agreements of all sorts bind us. It should be obvious therefore, that our own small individual wills are as nothing in this whirlpool. And if you add to that the thoughts of plants, animals, and rocks, of the planets and interplanetary forces, of the unfathomed activities in the unseen, even the whole humanity does not appear to be so great compared with the Universe.

This should teach us true humility. Also it should teach us resignation, but there is a true and a false resignation. The false is fatalism; the true is not to be bound by any restrictions to seek freedom by finding full scope for the spirit outside of these material and mental bonds. This in itself will help the world more than anything else. Thus we can become a *Bodhisattva* or *Nabi*.

MAY 2

The truth need not be veiled, for it veils itself from the eyes of the ignorant.

Their eyes are veiled because the ignorant are concentrated upon the dense earth and the gross vibrations of the Universe. Consequently they cannot see the finer atoms and vibrations, to which they are blind by custom, even as one who had been a cave dweller would not at first be able to distinguish objects in the light, and even as the infant takes some little while to peer distinctly upon the earth objects.

MAY 3

No one should allow their mind to be a vehicle for others to use;
one who does not direct one's own mind lacks mastery.

This has four aspects, three of which correspond to the three *Gunas* of the Hindus, the fourth of which is the diabolical condition where one controls and uses the mind of another. This is possible through hypnotism, black magic, and other practices.

Some people unknowingly and unwittingly become controlled by others. When there is love it does not matter much, but when there is not love it brings terrible consequences. The Sufis through their spiritual control of breath not only can protect their own minds but can guard the minds and hearts of others. Those who serve the Spiritual Hierarchy in higher capacities can protect even large areas in this way.

Those who are subject to emotional control, who are led by others in the mob, may be considered as *tamasic*. They are blind, ignorant. The *rajasic* ones escape the control of others, but their minds direct their will, and thus their real self is not free. This freedom is only true of the *sattvic* ones, whose inner spirit guides their vehicles. This means not cessation of thought but mastery of thought, so that one may refrain from or adhere to thinking just as one partakes of food or drink. The real spiritual fast is to refrain from thinking through concentration upon God; this is called awe-full contemplation—*Mushahida*.

MAY 4

Rest of mind is as necessary as rest of body,
and yet we always keep the former in action.

This is the besetting sin of life and there is no sin as great as this sin. It is the very source of all sin. And what is sin? It is lack of attention to God. If you study the commandments of Moses and the spiritual commandments of other religions, you will discover that the very central point in all these religions is the worship or love for that Being beyond all limited being. It is only in the sphere of limitation that there is error, that there is deceit, that there is heedlessness, that there is sin.

How then can one escape sin? By rising above this limitation, by ceasing to keep the mind in perpetual motion. When the body overeats, the blood is drawn to the stomach and digestive glands, and the rest of the system is kept poor. This is exploitation. But this is even more the case when the mind is overactive either in retrospection, direct thought, or imagination. Then the blood is drawn to the brain, and the rest of the system is exploited for the apparent benefit of mind. But this is not so and there is no benefit of mind, for you can build a beautiful roof on a house with a poor foundation and that is the most vain and expensive enterprise, for it is totally wasteful. Sooner or later the house will fall and that beautiful roof will only prove vanity.

Now mind is an instrument, an agent, not an actor, and if treated as a servant it can become most powerful. For this the practices of meditation and concentration are necessary, and no mind can become so powerful as that one disciplined by spiritual control.

MAY 5

Those who have given deep thoughts to the world are
those who have controlled the activity of their minds.

Just as continual attention to the body draws our interest from the life in general to ourselves in particular, so continual attention to the mind attracts us toward our thoughts and away from the world. But since this condition is more subtle, we do not see that by this we live in a world of our own creation. We send out vibrations and we give them a value—which is not a real value but one coined by these very vibrations.

Nothing has any value except by a universal standard of measurement. The wise therefore seek this universal standard and find that it is only discovered when their own thoughts are laid aside and measured in comparison with the thoughts of others and with the vibrations of the Universe in general. To do this, it is found necessary to control all activity of mind, then to determine what actions are valuable and important, and then to make each function of the mind purposive and profitable. This means to employ mind and not permit the mind to employ the self falsely.

MAY 6

Unity in realization is far greater than unity in variety.

This Unity is the greatest achievement conceivable. As a matter of fact, it is most difficult to find this unity in variety. There are sounds insects make that the human ear cannot hear; there are many vibrations of light and energy the eye does not appreciate and the instrument of one's ear cannot measure, for they are so delicate and they are continually being discovered. This shows that although there may be a unity in variety it is not always apprehended even when most appreciated.

As soon as the mind is quieted one finds the real cosmic vibrations which flow through the human heart and are even touched by and in the bloodstream. When one finds the blood mentioned in the Bible and Upanishads and Qur'an, it is because there is a tremendous significance there. For it is the heart and blood that keep the body a unity, and it is the love of God that keeps the Universe as a unity, which would otherwise be chaos. It is even said that when Parabrahm retains his breath the Universe is destroyed. This means that absence of God constitutes destruction—true alike of the Universe, ourselves, and our thoughts and emotions.

MAY 7

The afterlife is like a gramophone: the human mind brings the records;
if they are hard, the instrument produces harsh notes;
if beautiful, then it will sing beautiful songs.
It will produce the same records that one has experienced in this life.

So much attention is paid to the mind in the earthly life and consequently it absorbs all the vital energy. This in itself hastens the disintegration of the physical body, and also increases the potential life in the mental sphere, *Malakut*. Years upon years of habit produce idiosyncrasies between the atoms of the body of far more lasting nature than the body itself. So strong are the thoughts of some people that it takes ages to adjust them to the universal harmony.

The condition that takes place after the disintegration of the physical body is only different from this earthly condition in that there is no longer the gross body to impede activity and progress. After the body's disintegration our thoughts and wishes shape themselves much more quickly; they are more pliable. This enables one to achieve results in far less time even though the life is very, very much longer; by this is heaven or hell shaped, not created, but shaped out of the sphere.

This makes it appear that we have will-power, even tremendous will-power, but it is not so. What is true is that the concentration of desire always controls thought vibrations. We cannot see this while on earth because of the denseness of earth; in the mental sphere we see it and apparently control it. But it is nothing but the operation of law there. We see the law directly in that sphere, whereas it is hidden beneath the gross matter in this sphere where it also works but operates much more slowly.

MAY 8

Those who depend upon their eyes for sight, their ears for hearing,
and their mouths for speech, they are still dead.

Now the nature of the nerve is very wonderful, for every nerve is a conductor of mental energy, which gives it power over all kinds of physical energy. That is what the eye can see, but if there were no skull all brain would be eye. Similarly all brain would be ear, for every part of it can appreciate sound (although not, perhaps, exactly in the same way the specialized organ called the ear does). In fact, sensation and mind cannot be separated, but each sensation is a particularized function of mind. Nevertheless the particularization or specialization is a sacrifice of mind for some purpose; that special purpose is in turn to enhance the general purpose of mind, which is to be a vehicle of life itself.

Mind sees far beyond eye and hears far beyond ear. It is by this that such sciences as astronomy and geology have been built. But there is still a higher function of mind which enables it to see into things, and learn more than is on the surface only. It can penetrate into things, for what are things? They are the result of interactivity of mind-stuff and matter-stuff. They are the creatures of mind, and unless mind is greater than its own creations, it is failing in its purpose.

MAY 9

We cover our spirit under our body, our light under a bushel;
we never allow the spirit to become conscious of itself.

That is to say, so long as the spirit is considered "our spirit," so long as body is considered "our body," so long as light is considered as our possession, our attribute, this continual thought of self, prevents the Divine Spirit—**the** spirit, not **our** spirit—from becoming conscious of itself. We are afraid that if we let go this thought of self, we have completed our destiny; yes, we have completed "our" destiny, but that completion is the very thing which makes it possible for the Divine Spirit to manifest through us. This is the beginning of life, not the end of it.

MAY 10

When we devote ourselves to the thought of God,
all illumination and revelation is ours.

For it is the thought of God that obliterates the thought of self, as light coming into a chamber terminates darkness. It is the practice of *Wazifa*, *Darood*, *Fikr*, *Zikr*, and *Shagal* which bring revelation—not any philosophical consideration of them, but the actual practice. This can only be understood through the experience.

MAY 11

God-communication is the best communication that true spiritualism can teach us.

Ordinary spirit communication does not take us beyond name and form. It may take us forward in time but it does not take us out of time; it may take us backward in space but it does not take us out of space. In fact, it attaches us even more to conditioned existence. Besides, it does not develop the personality. It may add to our store of knowledge, but this is "our" knowledge, not the divine knowledge, and this becomes an additional weight to the spirit which is further buried under debris just so long as we dwell in the realm of finitude.

MAY 12

The mystic desires what Omar Khayyam calls wine—the wine of Christ,
after drinking which no one will ever thirst.

This is the love of God which appears as manifestation in *Djabrut*, that is to say, the sphere of heart. Even on the earth plane it flows with every heart-pulsation. It is that which keeps us alive here and which keeps us alive hereafter, and which impelled us heretofore on our way to manifestation. It is that which everyone desires, which is all joy and happiness. It is that which constitutes all delight of Paradise. And what is that? It is nothing but Allah in the manner in which He presents Himself to His creatures. Practice of *Zikr* brings it to us here and now. Every intoxication of soul is nothing but this wine, and it cannot be compared to any human delight.

MAY 13

Our limited self is a wall separating us from the self of God.

All spiritual training and discipline has no other purpose than this, to escape from this limited thought of self, to rise above the mind-mesh, to become free from all limitation. It is our own thought of self which confines us to limitation. Laying this aside, we lay all burdens aside. Do not try to cease to think of self; think of God and let that thought draw all other thoughts. This is the way to liberation.

MAY 14

The wisdom and justice of God are within us, and yet they are far away,
hidden by the veil of the limited self.

That is to say, laying aside this "I," all else is ours. Whatsoever we cease to consider our own, it becomes our own, and whatsoever we continue to call our own, that we do not possess, rather does the thought of that possess us.

MAY 15

One who looks for a reward is smaller than one's reward;
one who has renounced a thing has risen above it.

We can be no larger than our possessions. As Jesus Christ has said: seek ye first the kingdom of Heaven and all else will be yours. That is to say, cease to think particular thoughts, cease to have narrow attachments, desires, and ideals. Put your heart on the All, and the All will manifest Its Heart to you.

MAY 16

The poverty of one who has renounced is real riches compared with
the riches of one who holds them fast.

Real wealth, even from the material standpoint, is measured by the profits one gains from life when the resources are greater than the liabilities. There is a great truth in it, for if one has many possessions but has greater liabilities, one is in reality poor either from the standpoint of accounting or metaphysics. One may become bankrupt either in the world's court or in God's court.

Now those who have surrendered the things of the world by that gain mental control over the world. They have what they want and need and do not have what they do not want or need. If one diminishes one's wants, one will suffice with less, and if this sufficiency gives one everything one desires and requires, one is wealthy. While the holder of riches, who must give thought to the riches, does not own them—he or she is only a holder.

Likewise, one who has renounced the knowledge of the world has all knowledge, for the heart can then peer into the mind of anyone and take from the sphere whatsoever it needs. This gives it all wealth, wealth of knowledge, wealth of culture, wealth of beauty, wealth of power, wealth of possessions in name and form. All these belong to the one who belongs to God.

MAY 17

*Love for God is the expansion of the heart, and all actions that come
from the lover of God are virtues: they cannot be otherwise.*

That love for God is the expansion of the heart is a truth; in fact, it is **the** truth, for the heart delighted with itself, the heart which does not sympathize with others, is no heart, it is a stone. When the heart expands, it moves in sympathy with all the spheres, so that its activities are in harmony with the Universe. This is what the Buddha called "Right Action," which springs from compassion. Out of this all virtues arise, for all are of the nature of compassion but are considered as so many different virtues by the cognizing mind.

MAY 18

God is the ideal that raises humankind to the utmost height of perfection.

If we regard the planes as located one above the other according to the fineness of their vibrations and substance, it can truly be said that attraction toward the God Ideal takes one into the sphere of the finest vibrations. From that point, the highest can be achieved by the casting away of all vestiges of self. This comes when one consciously and willingly unites with the Ideal. This is the highest condition, this is *Nirvana*.

MAY 19

*One is wise who treats an acquaintance as a friend; and one is foolish who treats
a friend as an acquaintance; and one is impossible who treats friends
and acquaintances as strangers—you cannot help this one.*

The supreme idea of friendship is that God is **the** friend, not a friend, but **the** friend. In other words, there is not friendship in any sense of separation, but in the sense of union, as of lovers. The wrong view of friendship is to think of it, to consider it at all with the discriminating mind. In this case, there is no real bond, there is attachment of *nufs*, and although no doubt this has an element of truth in it—no doubt there is a real bond between the two hearts—yet it is covered by the idea of self.

It is this which causes consideration of friend as "other" instead of regarding friend as "self." Consequently there is a line of demarcation caused by this discrimination, from the action of the *nufs* in making the heart-love submissive to the mind-thought. Therefore, the friend is not a confidant, but an acquaintance even when there is harmony of feeling.

And by the same law, when there is not harmony of feeling, one would consider the acquaintance as a stranger, in that there would be no confidence, no familiarity. Such a person is so under the sway of *nufs* that nothing can be done until the karmic activity brings such pain that he or she begins to awaken. And what is the cause of the pain? It is the breaking of a habit. This habit has made a groove on the mind and now that the groove cannot contain the life force, another groove is being made from the new experience, and this brings the pain. But the real pain is the separation of the heart from its beloved which is very great in this type of person. Consequently when such a one suffers it seems that the pain is greater than with anybody else.

May 20

Insight into life is the real religion,
which alone can help us to understand life.

Religion is not belief; religion is that which links us to God. And what is life? It is an aspect of God; it is the aspect that enables Unity to appear as diversity, which develops harmonies out of Universal Sound, which patterns mind-stuff and matter-stuff in molds of beauty.

Insight is different from perception in that perception deals with variety, and insight takes one toward Unity. It is the apprehension and comprehension of Unity which leads to the understanding of life. This is a process of the heart, not of the head.

MAY 21

The realization that the whole of life must be "give and take" is the realization of the spiritual truth and fact of true democracy; not until this spirit is formed in the individual can the whole world be elevated to the higher grade.

This is a realization; and how can this realization be obtained? It is the spiritual practices which free one from the sway of *nufs*. It is the *nufs* which takes. Christ has said, "Freely give, freely receive." This is the spiritual condition, and it is the attainment of this condition which spiritualizes the self and the collective humanity. Not the philosophy, not the moral, not the thought, not the belief, but the realization alone will elevate the human and the universe.

MAY 22

The perfect life is following one's own ideal, not in checking those of others; leave everyone to follow their own ideal.

You cannot digest another's food, so why try to digest their thought? There is no vicarious atonement. God has created each form and each object in order that God might come to realization through that form and that object. When another is checked, God is checked; when another is hindered, God is hindered. This is very different from guidance; guidance helps toward some goal, it does not hinder. In other words it promotes activity, and if that activity does not appear to be in the right direction to the one to whom it is offered, it is because that one does not really know the right direction or has not the power and insight to transmute their direction into right direction. Every direction is right if it leads sooner or later to the Divine Ideal.

MAY 23

Every person's desire is according to their evolution; that which they are ready for is the desirable thing for them.

You do not feed the plant upon that which is desirable for the animal nor give the bird the food best for the horse or dog. So it is with all humanity. The short person must take smaller steps than the tall person, and the educated person may be able to read more rapidly than the slightly cultured. The destiny of *nufs* is not destruction of *nufs* but transformation of *nufs*. This is through a tender and pliable and yet subtle turning and tuning, never through positive opposition, unless it is certain that the person is under control of diabolic forces, which is seldom. Even then the Sufis use *Wazifas* and other practices, calling upon God. As soon as one thinks of oneself as actor rather than agent one falls into the very pit one has dug for another.

May 24

Discussion is for those who say, "What I say is right, and what you say is wrong."
A sage never says such a thing; hence, there is no discussion.

Discussion is an activity of the discriminating mind; it is the offspring of *nufs*. Not even the Prophets discuss when they denounce or arraign. They may utter a diatribe but they do not argue. There are but two courses: to stand firm to the point of view of God, knowing it is the point of view of God or to reconcile so far as possible to the point of view of another without antagonizing the other. This last is the common action of the seer especially in dealing with an individual, no matter how wicked. The former should only be used in a general way to move the masses of humanity in time of great peril.

The fact is that the "you" is always wrong: I-ness and my-ness and you-ness and your-ness constitute the essence—if such it can be called—of what is wrong; it is the very nucleus of evil. But when one serves God one strives to lead others toward God, which is best done in a spirit of love and harmony. To criticize or admonish another to prove that one is right is never the habit of the Sufi.

May 25

Tolerance does not come by learning, but by insight; by understanding
that each one should be allowed to travel along the path
which is suited to their temperament.

It is from the view of God that real tolerance comes. This is the stage of the enlightened who understand all. If a person were all heart, he or she would find that they were also all eye. In *Djabrut*, if one can be said to have a body (let us call it a spiritual body), that body emits light and receives light from every portion of its surface. Its functions are not differentiated. Furthermore, as soon as one thinks of another, as soon as a person loves another, instantly they are as one. They may appear separate at other moments but then they are one.

This is hard to understand from the physical or mental points of view, for in these planes the life is very different; besides which, activity depends to a certain extent on our differences, even though these differences cause harmonies. Yet so long as there are differences there is the opportunity for disharmony.

The heart point of view of the sage is to regard all opinions as offspring of mind, and knowing that spiritual evolution is not a mental process—rather a sloughing of mind—it is not against any special opinion, thought, or belief that the sage is opposed, but against mental centering in itself. And the only way the sage can oppose it is to give all love and tenderness toward all people, regardless of opinions, knowing there is no such thing as right opinion and wrong opinion, that "opining" itself leads to difficulties.

MAY 26

So long as one has a longing to obtain any particular object,
one cannot go further than that object.

This is not wrong of itself. For instance, that longing leads to concentration—or rather when it does lead to concentration, when it is strong enough to keep one from flitting hither and thither, that longing cannot be called evil. From this point of view not even passion is wrong if it keeps one concentrating on the same point of passion. It becomes wrong when it leads to unsteadiness, to satisfaction of self, and to lack of consideration toward the object desired.

If all objects are considered as living, whether they are the work of human hands or of God's, already the seed of unity is sown. It is only after one has come to the realization that any particular object will not bring happiness or satisfaction that one is ready for the next step. Therefore the sage may not oppose that which seems to lead toward vice; it is not vice in itself which is vicious, it is the constant tendency toward diversity, the lack of constancy, the absence of any motive or concentration in life which is wrong.

Therefore Sufis always help others to select some ideal, as the others must choose something they desire or love, so as to form a bond of attachment. Then they can learn concentration, collection of powers, gaining a purpose or motive in life. The highest morality, without this concentration, may lead nowhere. But the simplest undeveloped soul, once gaining a purpose and concentration, will advance far on the journey toward the goal, often unaware that he or she is traveling.

May 27

One's path is for oneself; let everyone accomplish their own desires
that they may thus be able to rise above them to the eternal goal.

Every soul on the journey toward manifestation selects certain qualities out of the Empyrean, so to speak, which form the nexus of their later desire. This is the seed of a person's nature and it is through the development of personality—not its suppression—that the fulfillment of the involution and evolution is accomplished. As the very nature of desire was born out of unfulfilled love, it is not proper to crush this desire entirely—to transmute it is the right procedure.

From one point of view all desire is crushed, but from another point of view this is not so. What is necessary is to demonstrate through life itself that satisfaction cannot arise out of any particular thing; rather that satisfaction only comes from the *Pleroma*, the totality of thing-ness, not from the things themselves. And what is this *Pleroma*? It is nothing but an aspect of Allah, the aspect which satisfies every soul.

May 28

The control of self means the control of everything.

That is because this control leads to the *Pleroma*, the fullness of things, the essence of thing-ness, and so includes everything. Each thing, which can be called a separate thing, has a *nufs* that distinguishes it from other things, but this distinction is on both sides: both the thing and the desirer of that thing must have the *nufs*. The chemist can control atoms by destroying the *nufs*, and the seer controls mental atoms in much the same way. In that way you control all thought by destroying the *nufs* of thought.

May 29

God is love; when love is awakened in the heart, God is awakened there.

That is to say, one realizes that the real experience of life is, was, and shall be nothing but God. We are nothing but God's dreams of self until we awaken to the fullness of the true self.

May 30

All the disharmony of the world caused by religious differences is the result of humankind's failure to understand that religion is One, truth is One, and God is One; how can there be two religions?

As religion is **the** connection between the human being and God, and as that connection designates unity, there is no room for two connections. Whatever be one's relation toward God, it is a single relation and a singular relation. One can no more foist that relation on another than one can make one's parents the parents of another. To each soul God may appear different, but it is the appearance which is unique, not the reality. All we can understand is that appearance. As God appears to us so shall we understand God, but neither can we give to another our eyes, our mind, nor our heart. These things distinguish us one from another and cause the apparent differences in religion, which are nothing but these different points of view in their appearances as different religions.

May 31

The use of friendship for a selfish motive is like mixing bitter poison with the sweet rose syrup.

Friendship is born of the higher self; it is the reflection of the love of God. In other words, it is light itself turned in a certain direction. But selfishness is the product of shadow, and when light or color is mixed with shadow either the light is dimmed or the color marred.

JUNE 1

One's bodily appetites take one away from one's heart's desire;
one's heart's desires keep one away from the abode of one's soul.

The first of these lessons is easy to understand yet difficult to attain. For among the desires of the body are not only those lusts which seem to drag us downward, but even more so the great attractions of life—pleasant music, scenery, art, poetry, handsome people. There is in them the essence of ideal, the true nature of ideal. It can even be said that the very lusts of humanity are shadows of good things, and it is due to the warped nature and sway of the *nufs* in darkness that brings such frustration about. But for the most part it is clear to the mureed that the sway of the bodily appetites hold one back from one's heart's desire, and one learns from Murshid the means to eradicate their dominance from one's system.

The desires of the heart are more subtle. Is not beauty desirable? Are not beautiful things desirable? Do we not need objects or thoughts in which to express the inmost being of the soul? Yes, we may need objects for the inmost expression, but there is another aspect of life which is neither expression nor suppression which comes when God fulfills the Divine Purpose in the human, which of itself is the very fulfillment of humanity's purpose in life.

Even the highest ideal, the greatest harmony, the most valuable things in the Universe, one must be willing to sacrifice if one is to find the true spiritual life, the life of God in God. For that, one cannot stop even with heart, which stands as a globe over the soul; for in heart there is not full completion of Unity. Until all desires have amalgamated into the desire for God, the soul's desire to return to its source, the object of the journey has not been attained.

JUNE 2

Words are but the shadows of thoughts and feelings.

The nature of feeling is light; the nature of thought is the tenor and tuning. Words are means for objectifying these thoughts and feelings in the material world. Thoughts and feelings are therefore materializations and are of the nature of shadow. So are words, only words come in the form of vibrations, which affect the ears and brains and do not appear as sense-objects. Yet for this sphere and for the cosmos, they are of the nature of shadow.

JUNE 3

The more elevated the soul, the broader the outlook.

The teaching of the Upanishads is that the *Atman* is located in the center of the heart, which is the smallest of things and yet it is also the largest thing in the Universe—if indeed it can be called a "thing." To understand this better it must be explained that there are at least two categories of words: those which define or describe what the mind can perceive and conceive and which are by nature finite (or occasionally indefinite) and those which belong to the infinite and unfathomable, for which words are used not as definitions but as symbols. Such is the type-form of the term "soul."

Yet there is a truth in this teaching of the Upanishads from another point of view which can be called esoteric. That is to say, the more one concentrates upon unity, the smaller the apparent field of compass in the concentration, the greater becomes that outlook although the channel is narrow. It is like making a telescope more powerful albeit its range of vision is narrow.

At the same time, soul not being dominated by space is also quite unlike a telescope for it has an action like a fan opening more and more, and in the process of concentration there is both greater range of vision and greater depth of vision. This is beyond sphere of mind, also beyond heart, for soul of itself can attune itself to anything and everything that is.

JUNE 4

The secret of a friend should be kept as one's own secret;
the fault of a friend one should hide as one's own fault.

From the Sufi point of view friendship means a union, and at the very least this union should transcend the realm of mind and thought. Do not consider friend as friend, consider friend as self. This is the condition in *Djabrut* where lovers are as one being. This is not to be confused with "soul-mate;" there is no "soul-mate" and all the members of the Spiritual Hierarchy form the single embodiment of One Master in a condition beyond *Djabrut*, called *Lahut*, which is inconceivable to mind.

Now the truth is that all planes interpenetrate, and for the earth plane it means that all principles operate here now. That is to say, what is true above must be practiced below if we want to bring God-Wisdom to earth. So in considering friend as none other than self, the critical faculty is never used even though in that process one may also have to cease praising the friend. In other words, remove all thought and analysis from the scene. This leads to negation of mind, which helps to blot out the fault of another by never referring to it; this does not acquit another, but it helps to help them.

JUNE 5

Forbearance, patience, and tolerance are the only conditions
which keep two individual hearts united.

These are the heart faculties, which flow out of the heart naturally and do not have to be cultivated. This is the difference between the moralist and the sage. The moralist tries to pour into the heart what the sage knows to be there already. It is heart, not head, which holds these qualities, and the awakening of heart brings them to view.

June 6

We blame others for our sorrows and misfortunes,
not perceiving that we ourselves are the creators of our world.

This blaming comes from habit, a habit we cannot readily blame in others for it is the way of the world. At the same time, when one overcomes such a habit it is often to fall subject to blame at the hands of others even without ever blaming others. The Sufis call this the path of *Malamat* or blame.

It is the limited outlook of *nufs* which causes all difficulties. Events of themselves are neither good nor evil. It is the light which makes day and the darkness which causes night, and this is also true of the affairs of life—that when the mind is illumined there is no longer anything which can be called evil. What is usually termed evil is due to the ignorant sway of the *nufs*; for it is ignorance which is the source of selfishness, which in turn creates all disharmonies and evils in the world. The world does not create them; the false self molds them out of the world.

June 7

Nobody appears inferior to us when our heart is kindled with kindness,
and our eyes are open to the vision of God.

Inferior and superior are qualities connected with dualism. Heart knows only oneness, and therefore heart does not understand distinctions into grades. The sun looks upon the earth—not upon the hills and mountains and valleys and oceans. From a certain point of view these things exist; from another point of view they cannot be perceived. So it is with the outlook of the heart; when it sees God, it perceives all in the light and this of itself brings to fruition kindness, compassion, and all heart qualities.

June 8

Selfishness keeps one blind through life.

For it is *nufs* alone which limits one's vision. Not all the education, morality, or external processes can alter it; for until one becomes unselfish one is lacking in great understanding.

June 9

The final victory in the battle of life for every soul is when one has risen above the things which once one most valued.

To give up material things for intellectual knowledge, to surrender worldly knowledge for the compassion and wisdom of the heart, to discard the compassion and wisdom of the heart in the assimilation within God—the eternal, everlasting, and ever-present existence—these are all steps on the way. In other words, once an ideal is attained, it must be dropped in order that a higher ideal and a further goal may be attained. So there is nothing which can be explained, discussed, or put into words which may not have to be discarded. Even our highest principles and morals can become obstacles if they hinder the spiritual freedom which God and God alone can bestow.

June 10

When power leads and wisdom follows, the face of wisdom is veiled and she stumbles; but when wisdom leads and power follows, they arrive safely at their destination.

Wisdom and power are not necessarily two things; they both indicate control, only what is known as power is control over or through the stuff of creation, the coarser vibrations from which matter-stuff and mind-stuff have sprung. Control of these atoms and vibrations is called mastery.

By wisdom is meant the view of Unity, which comes from the growth of insight. Through insight one can always gain power, but power does not take one beyond the sphere of activity. By wisdom one can control the lesser through the greater and overcome the forces of mind through heart and of matter through mind.

JUNE 11

One's whole conduct in life depends upon what one holds in one's thought.

This has various aspects. For instance the whole material life is dependent upon mental faculty. This is proven by the fact that without nerve-energy, there could be no muscular motion; it is even clearer when we examine sense-activity and still more when we consider the intellectual aspects of life.

Concentration is a process by which will masters mind, and this leads to a greater collectivity of mental power which can be adapted to whatever purposes are necessary or advisable. But there is another stage which comes when one abandons this mastery. Through the abandonment of particular faculties of mind, one may advance into the Buddhic stage. Then the mind becomes as a garden which may be planted and sown, just as a physical garden may be planted and sown. And as one need not identify oneself with matter-stuff, neither is it necessary to identify oneself with mind-stuff, although it may appear to many that the intellectual life is the basic life.

Moral qualities appear when the heart is opened, which comes spontaneously through the abandonment of identity with mind-stuff, which of itself sloughs off the vestiges of the false ego.

JUNE 12

They who can be detached enough to keep their eyes open
to all those whom circumstances have placed about them,
and see in what way they can be of help to them,
it is they who become rich;
they inherit the kingdom of God.

It is abandonment of the fruits of action which gains control over all action. This is a puzzle which is presented in the Bhagavad Gita, and it remains a puzzle so long as value is placed upon the individual ego. It is true that in a certain sense there is an ego and individuality, but the development of the personality comes not through any stress upon this individual-ego, but from the opposite course. The personality receives its full development from the acquisition of attributes. This faculty is limited by thought-power, which does not add to the faculties one has already although it may strengthen any and all of them. To secure another faculty, one must appeal to the source of all attribution—which is God.

So long as one points to anything—physical possession, intellectual attainment, friends, acquisitions, or attachments of any kind—that means separation also, separation from everything not included in these acquisitions and attachments. When no difference is made between what one has and what one has not, accommodation is created for infinite attainment for then no door is closed upon anything in the universe, and one becomes as the very custodian of God's gifts.

JUNE 13

True justice cannot be perceived until the veil of selfishness has been removed from the eyes.

So long as *nufs* has control there is not a balance, there is not observation of law, and certainly there is no pure love. For during that condition when *nufs* has control, all events are related to a thought—whether such events have any actual connection with that thought or not—and a set of relations is substituted for a set of actualities. Justice, mercy, all morals, and all wisdom are the natural aspects of a life undeterred by these false relations.

JUNE 14

Our thoughts have prepared for us the happiness or unhappiness we experience.

In the first place, thoughts divide experiences between pleasant and unpleasant. By thinking of something as pleasant, one creates at the same time the thought of what is not pleasant. That is to say, there is dualism; there are two thoughts instead of one thought. Whenever the discriminating mind operates, the thought is double; it has two aspects which may be called good and evil, pleasant and unpleasant—these are the fruits of dualism.

All the great prophets have described God's Kingdom as a place or condition where there is no day and night. That is to say, it is a sphere of universality, all inclusiveness. When one abandons the fruits of self-action, action is not abandoned but there is no attachment to qualities. Consequently, overcoming an existence which is conditioned in any way, one attains to a state of bliss which leads to highest cultivation of mind.

JUNE 15

Love is the best means of making the heart capable of reflecting the soul-power;
and love in the sense of pain rather than of pleasure.
Every blow opens a door whence the soul-power comes forth.

This love means the abandonment of *nufs*; it means self-sacrifice. By it all the fruits of separated individualism are eschewed. The pain of love comes from the breaking of a habit or an attachment, and this always brings pain, but that is only the external aspect of it. If there were no energy or power, there could be no pain, and the better we are able to withstand pain, the greater the spiritual power we can exhibit. This growth of the spirit is only possible through esoteric training or through prolonged suffering, and the first is always greatly to be preferred, for without destroying, it enables us to live through it.

JUNE 16

Every experience of the physical, astral,
or mental plane is just a dream before the soul.

For in the experience of these planes the experience is not of our self. It may arise from thought of self, but the experience is not our self—actor and action are two, not one. What is this world? What are these thoughts, these sensations, these habits, these longings, these desires? They are the externalizations of the inmost spirit taking form in the matter-stuff and mind-stuff of the universe. Without that Supreme Self dominating the whole scene of creation, there would be no experiences, and it is because of the God in us, which is our very essence, that we do have experiences, but they are still fantasies of a mighty Being which the finite mind cannot comprehend.

JUNE 17

The fire of devotion purifies the heart of the
devotee and leads to spiritual freedom.

Devotion is a concentration and every concentration leads to the attainment of some desire or some ideal. But devotion is also a quality devoid of self; it leads to the abandonment of self and therefore it has the effect of purification.

JUNE 18

When love's fire produces its flame, it illuminates like a
torch the devotee's path in life, and all darkness vanishes.

This is not something to be understood by material events or physical or mental reflection. It is a natural condition and Sufis attain to it through practice of *Zikr*. *Zikr* collects the atoms and arranges them in such a way that the atoms send out their sparks of vibrations and so increase the energy within and around one. It is a natural process, and what affects these atoms also in time affects the atoms and cells of the body and in turn these benefit the mind and heart. Great are the wonders of *Zikr* discernible only to the *Zakir*.

JUNE 19

It is mistrust that misleads; sincerity always leads straight to the goal.

Mistrust is of the nature of dualism. Setting forth in no direction, having no particular ideal or aim, mistrust cannot lead to any goal. Therefore the wise do not enter in relations with those whom they do not trust except in such a way as to bring spiritual benefit to either or both parties. When one has no trust in another, it is better to abandon the act entirely unless one can do it oneself. Success in the spiritual life does not consist in the attainment of any particular objects or qualities, but in mastering the processes which lead to successful attainment.

June 20

Love lies in service; only that which is done not for fame or name,
not for the appreciation or thanks of those for whom it is done, is love's service.

The great pity is that so many acts that are done out of real kindness have been interpreted to mean the existence of goodness of personality. Personality, name, and fame are all of mind-nature; they are not of heart-nature. They are of mind-nature, and to ascribe goodness or kindness to mind is contrary to truth and also out of harmony with the teachings of the Holy Ones. Jesus Christ has said that God alone is good, and Mohammed called God the Beneficent, the Merciful.

Love is far more abiding, far more real than name or fame or even personality from a certain view. All things that are discrete things change form, pass away, and are not forever abiding. That which is attached to name and fame can only be self-love. Even if tinged with goodness, kindness, or piety, it lacks vision and contains the seeds of its own destruction. For where there is mind, where there is self and not-self, there is dualism, and where there is dualism there is evil. The self that is kind to another self can be unkind to the other self, but where love has broken the bonds of self, there can never be unkindness, never be cruelty.

June 21

The soul is all light.
Darkness is caused by the deadness of the heart;
pain makes it alive.

Soul is the *Nuri Mohammed*, the Universal Love-Light-Life, which becomes individualized in the heart. The heart covers the soul as a globe and in a certain sense cannot hide the light. But the heart has a movement like the expansion and contraction of a sphere from a point to a universe. It can contract until it is very tiny and expand until it is immeasurable.

Contraction of heart may result from one's outlook on life or one's experience of life. When the consciousness is attracted to outer things and becomes intoxicated thereby, the heart ceases to expand in its natural manner and this interferes with the light of the soul which cannot then touch the surface.

But the heart cannot forever remain in that state, and if it is not moved naturally to expand, life's experiences through the law of Karma sooner or later awaken it. In the physical body it is true that when a muscle has not been used for a long time any attempt to move it is accompanied by pain. This is a thousand times more true for any area or portion of mind, and also infinitely more true of the heart.

June 22

The quality of forgiveness that burns up all things
except beauty is the quality of love.

This love is that which removes the boundaries between self and self. When there is no longer a this-self and that-self, there can no longer be pain of separation. This brings about pure forgiveness—not something mental, not a changed attitude of mind, but a changed attitude of heart.

June 23

Each individual composes the music of their own life;
if one injures another they break the harmony,
and there is discord in the melody of their life.

The music of our being consists not only in the sounds or thoughts or feelings we have that are pleasant to us, but in the sounds or thoughts or feelings we have that do not cause pain to others. We have in life two relations—our relations to ourselves and to others. When we are ill or suffer in any manner this can be due to the injury we have done to ourselves, or the injury we have heedlessly permitted another to do to us. For the spiritual student the first is ignorance, the second heedlessness—so in either case no one else is to blame.

That is to say, once the heart is awakened we do wrong in allowing others to injure us and we do still greater wrong in injuring others. When the heart is pure, the thoughts will be pure, and the melodies of voice—whether sung or spoken—will be pure, the breath will be pure, the atmosphere will be pure, and God's Radiance flowing through the personality will bring peace.

JUNE 24

One who with sincerity seeks one's real purpose in life,
is oneself sought by that purpose.

The search is a tuning; spiritual development is a tuning. The law of concentration is that not only will, not only mind, are focused upon some particular goal, but the whole consciousness and breath are placed in harmony. This brings about attunement of self, and once this attunement is gained the greatest obstacle to obtaining any wish has been overcome.

Indeed there is nothing outside of us that stands very much in our way. There is so much in the Universe that everybody could easily be satisfied without harming others. Concentration of itself draws the desired thing, and peace and harmony within hasten its coming. This unity is the very purpose of our existence which includes all smaller purposes within itself.

JUNE 25

Through motion and change, life becomes intelligible; we live a life of change,
but it is constancy we seek. It is this innate desire of the soul that leads one to God.

No matter what our aim or object in life, its security does not bring us happiness. There is a constant struggle between our attraction toward joy and our attraction toward peace. This struggle causes our involution and evolution, and its end is not attained until the two are brought into equilibrium and coalesced. That is to say, the nature of God or *Nirvana* is not a dead-peace, but Life in its fullness, Love in its magnificence, Light beyond our conception. When we have tired of changing phenomena and seek God alone, we find that constancy, that peace, that joy.

June 26

Every being has a definite vocation and one's vocation is the light that illumines one's life. The one who disregards one's vocation is a lamp unlit.

That is to say, the root cause of our misery is our wrong attitude, and this comes mostly from our selfish outlook. The interesting thing about this selfishness is that while it may cause some harm to others—we may rob, steal, injure, or deceive others—the greatest and by far the greatest injury is done to the self. It is seldom if ever that one finds a happy rogue or thief. The very law under which they operate brings them poisoned fruit.

Repentance toward God which lifts one from the vestiges of selfhood is the one thing which will save humanity. If one has been a thief it may lead one to learn to be skillful, astute, wide-awake, faithful to one's profession, to acquire ability in concentration, and so develop many arts and faculties which can do one good. Those acquisitions are never lost, and whether one repents here, now, or hereafter, they will sometime help one in one's evolution. Only blinded by one's selfishness, one spends long years in the abuse of the Divine Attributes and so finds no satisfaction.

June 27

The heart sleeps until it is awakened to life by a blow; it is as a rock, and the hidden fire flashes out when struck by another rock.

Rubber is a very interesting substance to the spiritual student. It expands and has been used for balloons; it stretches, is pliable, is used for cushions to bring ease and comfort. But when subjected to extreme coldness it becomes hard, brittle, and useless.

In some respects the heart acts similarly. The heart in its ordinary condition expands and contracts, showing kindness outside and contracting its love within. But once it becomes cold, it becomes hard and useless. Often the delicate love of another has no effect upon it, and it may have to be rubbed hard, to be struck, to be smashed into bits. It is life itself which does this either through the agency of a more powerful though venomous personality, through a more powerful but kindly personality, or through the suffering of life itself.

JUNE 28

The awakened heart says, "I must give, I must not demand."
Thus it enters a gate that leads to a constant happiness.

Heart may not know, but soul contains all qualities, all attributes, all substances. When heart gives, it draws upon the infinite treasure of the soul but may not know that treasure to be the infinite. It is the expansion of heart which gives it life, the contraction dulls it. It is the expansion of heart which brings all joy, all harmony. It is this which comes through *Zikr* and *Fikr* when one realizes that the heart is the shrine of God, Who is All Love and Life and Light and Goodness.

JUNE 29

The worlds are held together by the heat of the sun;
each of us are atoms held in position by that eternal Sun we call God.
Within us is the same central power we call the light,
or the love of God; by it we hold together
the human beings within our sphere,
or lacking it, we let them fall.

Owing to the nature of the human mind, every attribute is given a different name; the result is that although an essence may have many attributes, the mind segregates them. Thus one of the qualities of love itself is warmth, fire, heat. They are not separate. In the physical world the cold metals are brittle; although their particles are closer together, the force that welded them is gone. When we wish to mix metals we heat them; when we bake cakes we unify the materials through heat. It is heat and love which tend always toward unity.

What is called gravitation, cohesion, and adhesion is nothing but aspects of the Universal Living Love-Light. In the three worlds, there is a focus of power which can be called the sun, in which and through which this universal power operates. If there were not this coordinated power there could be and would be nothing but chaos—no law, no rhythm, no beauty.

The cells of the body are held together by this same law, and by it, and according to it, human beings form societies. This teaching has been excellently worked in principle by Moses, more implicitly by Plato, and quite explicitly by Swedenborg. According to their own evolution each of these men interpreted it more or less. It is love-nature which holds people together; it supplies the magnetic power which draws the infant to the breast of its mother, the élan which attracts the sexes, and all motive and feeling leading toward unity, union, or harmony of every kind.

The very cells of our body no longer coalesce when we break the law. Neither do they hold together when, mastering the law, one learns how to dissolve this physical body. In that case there is a supreme concentration on the love of God and on service toward God which enables the soul to become free from the sphere of great limitation and rise to function in a sphere of much greater freedom.

The law of friendship, the law of love, the law of harmony is all one. Through the ego we lose this universal power, through willingness to surrender we gain it all.

JUNE 30

When one dives within, one finds that one's real self is above the perpetual motion of the universe.

Strictly speaking, above the mind-mesh there is only one self—call it *Atman, Dharmakaya, Ruh,* Soul, or what you will. It is our aspect of it that gives it a name—seeing partly from below the mind-mesh and partly from above through realization—but the reality in us is nothing but **That**.

July 1

Humanity's pride and satisfaction in what
they know limits the scope of their vision.

For this pride and satisfaction keep the attention on what one has, or has done, and not on what one might see, or do, or know. Without this egocentric condition there would be no limitation upon our faculties—human or super-human—if such a word can properly be applied to them.

July 2

One must first create peace in oneself if one desires to see peace in the world;
for lacking peace within, no effort of one's own can bring any result.

One may begin with the simplest processes of body—how to keep the body well, fit, and strong. In this one can learn the law of harmony and the laws of breath. These same laws will enable one to understand and utilize the mind; they will also enable one to understand and harmonize with the minds and hearts of others. It is the combination of law, which is universal, and the awakening of love, which distinguishes no self, that brings peace to the individual, the group, or the cosmos.

JULY 3

*The knowledge of self is the essential knowledge; it gives the knowledge of humanity.
In the understanding of the human being lies that understanding
of nature which reveals the law of creation.*

All human beings were made with essentially similar bodies, essentially similar mind-capacities, and essentially similar hearts. To understand one is to understand all. It is not necessary to dissect everybody's stomach either with the knife or with the analytical faculty of mind to understand nutrition. At best these give but a partial knowledge. The human body is a miniature cosmos and the human mind is a miniature super-cosmos if one only knew it, but until one understands one's own body and one's own mind one cannot understand the laws of relations.

Yet body and mind are not the self; these are but the outcroppings of self, which lies hidden deep beneath the vehicles with which it is clothed. All creation tends toward humanity, both the creation of the seen worlds including rock, plant, and animal and the creation of the unseen worlds—the elementals, *jinns*, and angels. All tend toward the human being in the highest expression of God.

JULY 4

*While some blame another for causing them harm,
the wise first take themselves to task.*

For the harmony of the wise can control even the world. To be a *Nabi*, one must relate every activity of the world to oneself and by one's control over oneself regulate or control the whole earth outside oneself. This is quite possible when a man or woman with heart surrendered to God undertakes to serve humanity without thought of self, refusing ever to discriminate between self and another, between self and non-self.

July 5

Whatever their faith, the wise have always been able to meet each other beyond those boundaries of external forms and conventions which are natural and necessary to human life, but which nonetheless separate humanity.

The truth of this, which is deeper than the historical or philosophical view, is that once the heart is open it can contact every other heart. There are not two sets of intuitions which conflict with each other. When the heart conveys an impression, it cannot be contrary to the impression carried to another heart. And when one has arrived at the state of heart-culture, all the hearts in the world are open to it.

This is the natural condition in *Djabrut*, but those who, because of their spiritual development upon earth, have recovered the faculties of angel and *jinn* can contact one another beyond space, beyond language, beyond mundane communication. This is natural for those traveling on the path to God.

They can even go further. Able to penetrate human hearts, they do not act or speak contrary to the beliefs of those around them except, perhaps, to carry them a step forward in their belief toward realization.

July 6

It is the message that proves the messenger, not the claim.

And this message finds its historical proof not in any acceptance of personality, although this is often the case, but in the events of the world. For instance, the Prophet Zoroaster has not been accepted by so many people as the other great prophets, yet the part that he played in history was very great, and that which he gave can never die.

July 7

Every soul has a definite task, and the fulfillment
of one's individual purpose can alone lead one aright;
illumination comes to one through the medium of one's own talent.

It is not necessary to turn the merchant into a musician or to compel the artist to be a mechanic. Perfection of any task leads to perfection of quality, and perfection of quality leads to realization of perfection in essence. This is the task of every soul together with the need to praise God every step of the way. All the metaphysics and theology are but the forms—higher or lower—with which teachings are clothed, but the teachings are Life itself.

July 8

While some judge another from their own moral standpoint,
the wise look also at the point of view of another.

By **some** is meant the people whose consciousness is still confined below the mind-mesh, who are in the *manasic* currents, who see only as their mind sees and have no vision further than the mind. But the **wise** have attained to the Buddhic condition, which enables them to see beyond name and form and so to look at life from every person's aspect of it.

July 9

While some rejoice over their rise and sorrow over their fall,
the wise take both as the natural consequences of life.

This shows that ordinary people are buoyed by the waves of life and rise or fall with them. They cannot understand the nature of life. The wise, keeping the rhythm of their breath steady and concentrating their heart upon unity, may be washed by these waves but never compelled by them to turn their course in life. They are above the pair of opposites and all duality in their vision of sublime Unity.

JULY 10

It is the lover of God whose heart is filled with devotion, who can commune with God, not those who make an effort with their intellect to analyze God.

All that is above the mind-mesh escapes analysis. Only what the mind can grasp and pull below can be subjected to such a process. It is like a fish pulling some substance from the surface into the depths. The fish could only understand what it has grasped, and the rest of the substance would escape its comprehension. So it is with Life and Truth. What the mind grasps is such a small portion of what really exists that unassisted mind can never unveil the mysteries. Yet when illumination comes through the awakening of heart, all things may be clear before the mind.

For this, no effort is necessary other than love, than self-surrender, than devotion, than throwing aside all these clinging thoughts. But you cannot tell the mind to love in a lesson nor the heart to love through a persuasive talk or talisman. The heart must love because it must love.

JULY 11

Do not bemoan the past; do not worry about the future; but try to make the best of today.

Paul said, "I die daily." By this one can escape Karma, especially if the heart keeps serene in its attraction toward God. The past that is bemoaned, the past that is prided belongs to the ego, to the *nufs*, and becomes the source of further misery. Whether it gave joy in the past or sorrow in the past, if it is carried along in the mind it will bring sorrow in the future.

Likewise, no thought should be attached to the future—"Take no heed for the morrow," as Jesus has beautifully put it. Each day is our great opportunity, each hour, and each breath. One cannot perform *Darood* with the mind far away in time or space.

July 12

The one who can quicken the feeling of another to joy or to gratitude,
by that much adds to one's own life.

The efflux of the heart is life and light and love, which the sentient mind comprehends as different substances, although they are just different attributes of the same cosmic substance. It is love that quickens the heart or self of another and love is life; therefore adding love is adding life. It is the same process and comes with the expansion of heart.

July 13

Praise cannot exist without blame; it has no existence without its opposite.

Praise from another may or may not affect us. If it affects us, if it buoys us up, it raises us. In Saum, saying "Praise be to God," the hands are raised, the thoughts are raised, the heart is raised, the voice is raised. This means a change of condition, and if there is a possible change of condition—a change upward—there can also be a change downward. Those who allow the words of others to raise them up, to intoxicate them, will also permit the words and thoughts of others to deject them, to intoxicate them in another manner. Either of these conditions is an intoxication; the person in a state of sobriety is one affected neither by praise nor by blame.

July 14

Riches and power may vanish because they are outside ourselves;
only that which is within can we call our own.

All the prophets have taught this, and urged humanity to cultivate this inner capacity. The hand can hold no more gold than it can seize, the mind can hold no more wealth or power than it can grasp; but there is no limit to the power, inspiration, and love of and in the awakened heart.

July 15

*The world is evolving from imperfection towards perfection;
it needs all love and sympathy; great tenderness
and watchfulness is required from each one of us.*

Those on the path of God need never expect kindness, cheerfulness, and friendship from others, nor need they hope for moral stability nor understanding on the part of those they meet. It is sufficient that the mureed understand that all love and goodness come from God, are signs of the presence of God, and that he or she praise God for every sign of God's Presence.

At the same time, all that is given to the mureed is for humanity not for his or her individual self. The marvelous spiritual magnetism which pours in and through the *talib*, the disciple on the spiritual path, reaches the whole of humanity for it enters the atmosphere of earth through the human breath and passes all around the globe. This breath is sustained by all the thoughts and feelings of tenderness and love. A single harsh thought of a master-mind can bring tribulation to multitudes.

July 16

*The heart of every person, both good and bad, is the abode of God,
and care should be taken never to wound anyone by word or act.*

If there were not some good in the human heart, life in the physical body would be impossible because the blood would be carrying poison to every cell and muscle and gland. We even see some strange deaths called heart failure, or given other names, which result from psychic poison impregnating the physical body.

Every harsh human thought immediately affects two fluids: the vital fluid or energy called "*prana*" which flows in and out with the breath, and the Universal Life-Love Essence which holds the very earth together, which is the heart energy. The harsh thought through *prana* affects chiefly the mind of another, for it is directed toward others. But such also is the nature of *prana* that the exhalation of the breath so operates that it touches the mental body of each person in its course, and whatsoever it gives to another it gives to oneself.

The effect of the heart-energy, which may be considered as the Universal Life-Force, is to strike every human being upon earth, even to affect others upon earth and those in the unseen. The proper use of this heart-energy is called *Ishk* by the Sufis, *Karuna* by the Buddhists, and *Agape* in the New Testament, which can be translated as "selfless love."

There is a difference here in that thoughts affect chiefly the thinker and the thing or person concerned in the thought, whereas the feeling of the heart-energy affects the whole cosmic body of Adam, the Universal Human. In this way, by our feelings and attitudes, we either raise or lower the whole humanity. So when Jesus Christ said, "Love ye one another," when Mohammed taught in the Qur'an that Allah created us from clots of blood, it was in reference to the fact—the great truth of existence—of the Universal Love-Energy.

The Master, the Saint, the *Bodhisattva* place their consciousness in this great stream, in this ocean of love, and by sending forth their thoughts of loving-kindness they benefit the whole humanity. When these thoughts are individualized they reach a few; otherwise they reach many. This is the reason for silence on the part of sages.

July 17

We should be careful to take away from ourselves any thorns that prick us in the personality of others.

The heart contains all notes, so consequently it can harmonize with any other heart. When there is disharmony, it is a condition of the head, and no matter how justified that disharmony, still it is related to *nufs*. God in the Supreme Essence contains all goodness and badness or none; that is to say God is the Perfection of quality, never its extension, no matter how great the extension be. God is not multitudes, or largeness, but infinite, and this infinite qualification escapes comprehension of finite mind.

If the spiritual aspirant keeps the breath in *Fikr*, if the *talib* holds the heart in *Ishk*, it is impossible to be unfavorably affected by others. One is either united with all souls or not so united. This does not mean condescension to others. It means either change yourself to become harmonious to that person, or else—with all the force at your command—to drive the evil spirit out of the other and make them whole. The use of this power is not contrary to *Ishk* if it heals another.

July 18

There is a light within every soul;
it only needs the clouds that overshadow it to be broken,
for it to beam forth.

Clouds are caused by mind, by thought of self and by nothing else. Not those whom we meet, not those who cause us pain, not those who seem to stand in our way, cause this light to be hidden. The light is hidden within the heart of each one and nowhere else. It is awakened by pain, and therefore many of our enemies, many of the obstacles in life, instead of hindering the higher self-expression, do more to enable us to bring it forth than anything else in life. It is only when we escape the bonds of self—either voluntarily and gladly or through pain and tribulation—that this light comes to the surface.

July 19

The soul's true happiness lies in experiencing the inner joy,
and it will never be fully satisfied with outer, seeming pleasures;
its connection is with God, and nothing short of perfection will ever satisfy it.

All the experiences of the outer world may be the greatest hindrances or the greatest help, or they may neither hinder nor help. Pleasure stands in our way when we are so attracted toward pleasure that the heart is lulled to sleep. Pleasure also stands in our way when we become ascetics and so shun pleasure. In this condition we have escaped the material aspects of pleasure but may be more than ever bound by the thought of pleasure. Whether this thought be of a negative nature or a positive nature, whether we seek or shun, we are bound.

The soul does not seek, the soul does not shun. The soul is not concerned with thought. It is concerned with the experience of God and can find this without regard to pleasure. Any experience can lead to God. Any experience can increase the clouds over the mind and can harden the heart. It is only when all attachment to experience is abandoned—including all thought connected with the idea of attachment—that the soul can find its peace and rest in God, and be concerned with God no matter what the material or mental circumstances.

July 20

*Every blow in life pierces the heart and awakens our feelings
to sympathize with others; and every swing of comfort lulls us to sleep,
and we become unaware of all.*

Ishk, the life current flowing through the heart and permeating the blood, touches all souls. It is a marvelous law that many people, often harsh and unsympathetic, upon suffering great pain then begin to show sympathy and love toward others. This is because of the very nature of *Ishk*, *Ishk* which knows neither self nor not-self. So when heart is in *Ishk* it shows loving-kindness to all, not recognizing differences. This is the ideal condition of the traveler.

July 21

**A study of life is the greatest of all religions,
and there is no greater or more interesting study.**

What is religion? It is that which unites human and God. And what is that? It is *Ishk*. Is *Ishk* love? Is *Ishk* life? Is *Ishk* light? It is none of them and all of them. Without comprehension of *Ishk* we cannot understand light, we cannot understand life, we cannot comprehend love.

Knowledge of *Ishk* is called *Ilm* by the Sufis. This is the truest and highest knowledge there is, which may be called Love-Knowledge—not knowledge of love or love of knowledge but the absolute Union of the two. This is "the study" and "the religion" in the truest sense of the terms.

July 22

We can learn virtue from the greatest sinner if we consider them as a teacher.

If one were entirely wicked, one could not live. The poison we send out poisons ourselves also. Just as the radio attuned to a certain pitch sends out vibrations picked up by others while at that pitch, it also picks up its own vibrations. So it is with the heart of humanity. What touches another touches oneself. As long as there is life in another there is some virtue there.

The root of the word "virtue" means manhood, life-force valor, and strength. The idea of goodness attached to "virtue" comes from the activity of the human mind. Yet this was a splendid conception. Since virtue means possession of life-force, and life-force is identical with Divine Power, and Divine Power is goodness, virtue and goodness may therefore be identified. So if we can find some goodness in dark places, we can find it everywhere. God is not only in the heavens, God is in the hells also.

JULY 23

Warmth melts, while cold freezes.
A drop of ice in a warm place spreads and covers a large space,
whereas a drop of water in a cold place freezes and becomes limited.
Repentance has the effect of spreading a drop in a warm sphere,
causing the heart to expand and become universal,
while the hardening of the heart brings limitation.

This shows the operation of *Ishk*. The expansive effect of *Ishk*, altering coarser vibrations into finer ones, creates what is called spirit. Spirit and matter are one, but the force of *Ishk* is lessened as it is removed from its source, which is the Throne or Heart of God (*Arsh*). Through *Ishk* ice melts, flowers grow, animals gain strength, and all human power comes. So to conceive that "Allaho Akbar" has one effect and "Ishk Allah" has another is blindness, except that "Allaho Akbar" seems to touch the physical body more quickly and the heart more slowly while "Ishk Allah" touches the heart more quickly and the physical body more slowly. But in the end they meet, the purpose is the same—the spiritualization of the field of endeavor. When the Divine Breath and Divine Efflux touch a sphere, they bring life, love, power, and inspiration, breaking all hardness of heart, mind, or body.

July 24

There should be a balance in all our actions;
to be either extreme or lukewarm is equally bad.

Attachment to matter prevents the soul from finding its way, as it becomes lost in a maze of phenomena. Attachment to mind or spirit causes one to ignore the purpose of matter and the cause of creation. Everything placed before us is there to test us and also to give us opportunity to perfect ourselves, the situation, or the thing. This is impossible when one is lukewarm. The real spiritual attitude is to be detached and yet warm in one's heart.

July 25

Our spirit is the real part of us, the body but its garment. One would not
find peace at the tailor's because the coat comes from there; neither can the spirit
obtain true happiness from the earth just because its body belongs to earth.

Ishk keeps the parts of the body together, unifies the mind, coordinates the body, mind, and heart. *Ishk* brings joy and *Ishk* leads to peace. *Ishk* may be found in matter and yet out of matter. Without *Ishk* there could be no matter, yet the existence of *Ishk* is not dependent on matter. The spiritual life is the life in and of *Ishk*, in other words, of love. This is true here now, heretofore, and hereafter. The word *Logos* which appears in the New Testament is nothing but a variation of *Ishk*; only it includes in its meaning Sound, Breath, and Intelligence. The best translation for *Logos* is Intelligence—in Sufi terminology, *Ilm*.

July 26

Every purpose has a birth and death; therefore God is beyond purpose.

God is beyond purpose and God is not purpose, yet if there were no God there would be no purpose. *Logos* and *Ilm* contain the idea of intelligence. There is intelligence in purpose and intelligence beyond purpose because purpose operates through mind and mind alone cannot partake of the supreme joys.

JULY 27

Belief and disbelief have divided humankind into so many sects,
blinding our eyes to the vision of the oneness of all life.

Belief and disbelief are products of the finite mind, born of the *manasic akasha*, or mental field of accommodation. Disbelief is only a variation of belief according to a limited view, but the essence of belief and disbelief is the same. Yet belief, if founded on love or felt with love, can bring about the awakening of heart; this will free one from belief and disbelief both, bringing one to the gates of knowledge.

JULY 28

Spirit can only love spirit; in loving form it deludes itself.

Now spirit, which is the real existing substance, does not act like the material things, and yet its behavior is reflected in the behavior of all forms of matter. The change from spirit to matter is a process of congealing; in other words, it is a freezing or cooling effect which causes the vibrations to take on a coarser but hardier form. Nevertheless, as soon as they take on that form they are no longer receptive to the more attenuated pulsations of the spirit.

This play and interplay of the spirit sustains the whole universe, and everything, even the thoughts of humanity, and memory, is dependent upon it. Without it nothing would adhere to anything else. Spirit within matter holds particles together and spirit within mind holds thoughts together. That is why in concentration the thought must be held with feeling. By that both matter and mind are spiritualized and God is perceived in God's Creation.

July 29

To love is one thing; to understand is another;
one who loves is a devotee, but one who understands is a friend.

This is the difference between *Ishk* and *Ilm*. The devotee is intoxicated by the love and light of God and longs for nothing else but to be bathed in the Universal Spirit; that one is a devotee, and some times a saint. But there is another stage: to be bathed in this ocean, to drink of the cosmic wine and not be drunk. This is an ultimate stage of sobriety, the fruit of which is *Ilm*—the supreme knowledge or universal intelligence, possession of which makes one a sage.

The devotee, possessing *Ishk*, becomes nothing in the sight of God as he or she is non-existing in the Existent. But the sage, possessing *Ilm*, is as God in the sight of nothing—he or she is Existent in the non-existent. *Fana* describes the devotee in *Ishk*, and *Baqa* describes the sage with *Ilm*.

July 30

Among a million believers in God there is scarcely one who makes God a reality.

Yes, God is the reality in our thought, the reality in our reality. So far as there is any reality in thought and our view of reality, it is God. But this is only one thought among the myriads of thoughts our mind holds. Now if God is infinite, God cannot possibly be only one among many; for under such circumstances, no matter how we characterized God, God would not be infinite. To be infinite, God would not be affected in any way by our thoughts. Therefore the Reality of God is beyond any thought, and this Reality is possible to us when we cease to think about God and begin to love God.

JULY 31

The soul feels suffocated when the doors of the heart are closed.

It is a natural thing for the heart to expand and contract, to open and close. This is reflected in the movements of the physical heart. But it is very unnatural for the heart to remain closed, to be fixed. This always has its reaction upon the physical heart, which becomes harder, its movements less rhythmical, its pulsations tense, and its contents poisonous, destroying slowly the divine temple of the physical body.

When we look at this contraction from the standpoint of the soul—which is nothing but *Ishk*, nothing but God—the Divine Life-Energy cannot touch matter. It is thrown back upon itself, and that impedes what is called its evolution. Strictly speaking, soul cannot evolve, cannot change, but it can experience life on the surface or in the depths. To be free it cannot be limited, and when the door to the exterior is closed, suffering naturally follows, for the essence of joy is shut out.

August 1

Understanding makes the trouble of life lighter to bear.

We need not escape pains and pangs; these must be, so long as we carry a mind. But mind is not the abode of understanding, heart is the abode of understanding. Trouble will not cease with the opening of the eye of the heart, but the evanescent character of disturbance will make itself clear. So time alone is sometimes a healer.

Exercising a muscle may cause a pain or overworking a muscle may cause a pain, but the first kind of pain makes no impression on the personality because there is a purpose in it. It is in this sense, when there is a purpose in view, that every burden is as a load in exercise, and the pain does not cause anguish.

August 2

The same herb planted in various atmospheric conditions will vary in form accordingly, but will retain its characteristics.

One cannot change an apple tree into a date palm, nor is it necessary. Beauty is revealed through harmony, not through uniformity. Every thing, every form has its purpose, which is hidden behind the form and the experiences of that form. So the human heart contains the seed of life—which is love—and no matter how buried, it can never be entirely destroyed for it contains the Divine Essence.

In the spiritual training, this seed in the heart is awakened to life, and through meditation a happy atmosphere is provided which will permit its growth.

August 3

*Think, before envying the position of others,
with what difficulty they have arrived at it.*

What is the one with the worldly position? If he or she has not the supreme knowledge, they must look carefully, lest in an unexpected hour, they are blown like the chaff in the wind. What is the one with intellectual honor? If behind intellectual honor there is not sincerity and humility, a person will be thrown to earth with violence at some unexpected time.

Those who have climbed and climbed successfully have done so through the pains which the heart has received, opening it so it pours its life-blood onto the very ground. In the sight of God human honors are as nothing, and the love of a parent or friend or devotee, given unselfishly, supplies all the merit that is.

August 4

Life is what it is; you cannot change it; but you can always change yourself.

From the spiritual point of view this Life is infinite, subject to neither change nor influence of finite forces. It has its characteristics which have been enumerated or described by humanity, but this Life is more than its characteristics. It can never be changed; it can never be ended; it is eternal in every direction. *Ya Hayy!*

From the outer point of view, what is called life is the result of the composite Karma of all creatures working in the sphere of the higher form or mode of Life. That is to say, there is Life, which is entirely separated from the sphere of Limitation, and there is life in the bosom of which there is the action and reaction of all the minute forces of creation. Out of the second form of life comes darkness, tribulation, night, and all evil, but the higher Life is never affected by it, any more than the sun is destroyed by fog.

AUGUST 5

Life is a continual series of experiences, one leading to the other,
until the soul arrives at its destination.

There are three apparent aspects of life, they being apparent not real. The first is the complete *Pleroma*, the fullness of all things, which is God, which includes all others and touches them within and without, and yet the *Pleroma* is not touched by them, even as the sun is not affected by earth or clouds.

Then there is the life in creation—for creation or *prakrit* or nature could not be if there were not life. In its sphere of forms and forces, there is the interplay of mineral, animal, and vegetable worlds; into this arena one is drawn and becomes the prey of *samsara*.

Then there is life as viewed from the individual standpoint, regarding each soul as separated; this is the human point of view and stands between the other viewpoints. But this view is an illusion, and the whole purpose of human existence is to enable us to escape this illusion.

AUGUST 6

External life is the shadow of the inner reality.

Absolute life is of the nature of light. When Allah performed the Creation, Allah drew toward a center the highest vibrations to make, as it were, a greater abode of light. By this in-drawing, contractive movement Allah caused light to depart in certain regions causing an apparent sphere of relative darkness. By this process and within this sphere the grosser worlds were made. And humankind, when its turn came, entered into this abode to help restore the light, which had been temporarily withdrawn from it.

AUGUST 7

At the cost of one failure, the wise learn the lesson for the whole life.

There is only one failure—heedlessness toward God. There are no other failures. We fail because we are blind or ignorant, and when we are sincere that which appeared to have been a failure will prove later to be a test which came to prepare us for a much greater success than we would have dreamed about when that experience arose.

AUGUST 8

*The more you evolve spiritually, the further you pass
from the understanding of every human.*

Human beings are held within the change of limited experience or *samsara*. At best they contact the *manasic* stream in their mental sphere and rarely, if ever, trust to their intuitions. They coin their forms of logic and common sense, which mean nothing in eternity, often to justify their injustice and defend their iniquity. Their laws, being based neither upon Nature nor God, are subject to change, decay, and dissolution.

The wise, seeking the eternal verities, are bound neither by such logic nor such law. They may stand alone in the midst of the ignorant, but they know how to stand; they know the limits of ignorance, and they possess that knowledge which all, consciously and unconsciously, yearn for.

AUGUST 9

One word can be more precious than all the treasures of the earth.

This word is "Allah," although its forms are legion. It tells the heart what cannot be said or described; it tells one about form, thought, and ideal; it draws the very life-blood of the heart. Behind the cry of the *muezzin* is an eternal cry of God for the soul, and the soul for God. This is the lost word, the lost music, the lost chord. It is lost and yet not lost, for it ever resounds in our midst.

AUGUST 10

Narrowness is primitiveness; it is the breadth of heart that proves evolution.

Mind that excludes, mind that divides, mind that evaluates distinctions and differences is un-illuminated mind. The illuminated mind, filled with *Ishk* and possessed of *Ilm*, will see these differences, will recognize these divisions, will notice these exclusions, but will also perceive their beginning and their ending, their unimportance in the totality of things and the relation of processes to reality. All knowledge through analysis is relative; only the heart-born intelligence brings one to the Supreme.

AUGUST 11

It is simpler to find a way to heaven than to find a way on earth.

On earth there are so many forces, so many attractions that draw one to the right or to the left, illusions that cast one into misery, enchanting distractions that take one from the path. There is the constant struggle with the idea that success consists in dominating another, exploiting another, conquering another.

All this is the foolish play of the ignorant who in their ignorance cause so much misery. The whole idea of heaven is the existence of a world where there is love, cooperation, and plenty for all, where humanity can escape the limitations with which it is bound upon earth. Yet the ignorant do not know that this is possible of attainment while still upon earth.

When one exploits oneself instead of another, when one dominates oneself instead of another, when one conquers oneself instead of another, heaven will be brought to earth.

August 12

*It is God, who by human hands, designs and carries out
God's intended plans in nature.*

There are the three aspects in life: first, that spiritual life which is God in Divine Fullness, uncontaminated by darkness of any sort; second, the Nature which was born from the movement of contraction, which appears as a world of relative darkness and which is the nexus of material life. To draw matter back into spirit, humanity was created who becomes the play between these other two forces or aspects. Actually these two are not in opposition, but they appear so to humanity who is attracted by one or the other.

Out of humanity comes the third aspect, *manasic* or mental life, which is between the two others, and consists of an apparent mixture of light and darkness in which the former always predominates but does not entirely dissipate the darkness until the flood of the spiritual intelligence makes that possible. By such means God enters into the created worlds and restores to Himself that which He voluntarily deprived Himself of in love and self-sacrifice.

Actually this is not so. It is all a dream, but it is the only explanation intelligible to humanity.

August 13

The lover of nature is the true worshipper of God.

Nature is the aspect of God which includes names and forms. It is still the aspect of God, and the darkness in nature is only a veil to prevent the pure latent light from blinding the eyes of creatures incapable of gazing into it. Not only the seer or sage but many people feel this tremendous urge within nature; not only the mystic and pantheist but many of limited scope are stimulated by trees or mountains and rivers. This shows that there is in nature the same spiritual life which is in the soul of humanity, and in this love there is the call of soul to soul, God recognizing God.

August 14

In the country you see the glory of God; in the city you glorify God's name.

In the country it is God who reveals God's Self to us, but in the city it is humanity who must work to attain satisfaction. And it is the work that should bring satisfaction. By practicing *Darood*, by praising the name of God, one can bring beauty and love into waste places and darkness, but beauty and love appear naturally in the fields, forests, and meadows.

August 15

The pain of life is the price paid for the quickening of the heart.

Heart expands and contracts. The *nufs* tends to keep the heart in contraction and brings about its hardness. This arises from the illusion of life, for really *nufs* has no control on heart, yet heart becomes intoxicated in the midst of life and blindly follows. This brings about control of will by mind and creates an unending trouble for everyone.

To open the heart there is a constant pull, and this pull does bring pain. The pain is not necessary, the pull is. But if one has kept the heart closed, has not voluntarily searched for God, then the very purpose and nature of life will cause this pull and accompany it with pain. Even the law of Karma serves not to draw people into the abyss but to bring them to a realization of a higher purpose in life.

August 16

Words that enlighten the soul are more precious than jewels.

For such words can never pass away in the here and now or hereafter. Even if we consider that soul will exist in the midst of God without the covering of the heart or mind or body, then will those words rain down in mercy upon suffering humanity and aid others in their struggle for liberation. Thus every mantram helps not only the devotee but is valuable for every person—those on earth, those yet to come, and those already gone.

August 17

Love is the current coin of all peoples in all periods.

Without *Ishk* there would be no social order, no nation, no family, no union or cooperation between soul and soul. This is the very thing which attracts people one to another and is the most valuable thing in life—it being the essence of life itself. War, poverty, and suffering show the absence of it, and prosperity, peace, and happiness are signs of its presence.

August 18

Do not take the example of another as an excuse for your own wrong doing.

To the *talib* there are two ways for selecting an ideal, and they may not be different. One way is to follow some spiritual person who has gone before you, preferably but not necessarily a person who has been met on earth. The other way is to develop the intuitive faculty and listen to the heart within, knowing that it is truly the heart which is heeded and being positively sure you are not under the sway of *nufs*.

The difference between following *nufs* and following heart is simple. *Nufs* always speaks in terms of self and not-self; heart recognizes only principles and not personalities. By following the heart there can be no mistake, but one should not be attached even to principles.

August 19

Overlook the greatest fault of another,
but do not partake of it yourself in the smallest degree.

There are several manners for overlooking the fault of another. One way is often equal to condoning it or excusing it. While outwardly this may be done, the more a mystic may outwardly defend such a wrong doer, the more inwardly he or she must pray for or condemn that person. Otherwise one will be partaking of that fault oneself and will have to answer for it.

Another way is the heart view, which while not excusing the person, recognizes the person's limitation and knows positively the difference between the real personality and one's acting or reacting under conditions that are more or less trying. The heart recognizes the conditions and endeavors to free that person from the subjugation by these conditions. This is the real nature of overlooking.

However, one must be careful in doing this, for it is not in committing the same act that one is partaking of it but in defending another openly for such an act when one is not aware of all circumstances, that one partakes of it. Likewise if one wrongly condemns another of a sin, you are guilty of a sin. Both these attitudes come from the domination of mind by *nufs*, and of will by mind.

AUGUST 20

Cleverness and complexity are not necessarily wisdom.

These qualities come to one from subtlety of mind, from being able to turn thoughts in certain directions and to mold the mind-stuff, so to speak, like a potter molds clay. To do this is still to operate in the sphere of mind. Wisdom, on the other hand, pours down from the spiritual world into the mental sphere as a ray of pure light, brings life and illumination to the mind, and clarifies it all at once, regardless of particular influences and conditions.

AUGUST 21

The whole world's treasure is too small a price to pay
for a word that kindles the soul.

The whole world's treasures cannot be carried away, besides which the thought of them would become a terrific burden. The soul desires freedom, and even possession of a thing may become a bar to freedom. When there is worry, when there is undue solicitude, then there is pain, there is a burden, and there is no freedom.

So all worldly possessions and all intellectual accomplishments may alike become ideals or hindrances, and if there is any doubt, the doubt itself must be removed. It is love alone that opens the portals of joy. Besides, the treasures of the world pass away, but the soul that is kindled knows its immortal worth.

AUGUST 22

That one is living whose sympathy is awake;
and that one is dead whose heart is asleep.

The real life is not limited by thought or action. The real life is not qualified by mind or matter. The real life is not restricted because personality is subject to certain laws. And how does the real life express itself? The essence of life is in the heart and nowhere in the human being if not in the heart. Yet when once discovered in the heart it can be found in every particle of one's nature and makeup.

Without heart, the human is merely animal or less than animal; with heart one becomes as a god. The energy of heart is life itself and the heart awakened brings the life to the surface.

AUGUST 23

By our thoughts we have prepared for ourselves the
happiness or unhappiness we experience.

When there is no attachment to things or thoughts, happiness is the natural condition. Mind may begin by selecting conditions under which there is a greater relative amount of happiness, and as soon as it does this the other conditions have a lesser amount of happiness. This creates pain, suffering, and longing, and this longing is never satisfied until the heart is open.

Heaven and hell are one and the same, but the reactions to the experiences are different. Artist, scientist, artisan, and musician all are agents of good in the world, but if each had to work in the place of the other, instead of finding beauty they would find misery. This shows that mind is the root-seat of these various conditions of happiness or unhappiness.

AUGUST 24

*Put your trust in God for support and see God's hidden hand
working through all sources.*

For the *salik*, or sincere traveler on the spiritual path, this trust should be a verity—not a blind faith in chance, not an unfounded optimism, but a trust founded upon surety. There is a world of differences between such a view and fatalism. The *salik* in order to see God's hidden hand, must **see**, and not merely hope. Then through the awakening of the heart the *salik* discerns the spiritual forces in every part of the Universe.

AUGUST 25

Faith is the A B C of the realization of God; this faith begins by prayer.

Faith brings knowledge without intellection, without use of any limited personal mind. The heart knows because it knows, without any special explanation for this knowledge. In such prayer the object is to free us from the sway of self; God can give us this freedom and it is to this end humanity should pray. When one prays for conditions or things, one limits prayer, limits oneself, and deprives God from displaying God's Wisdom and Magnanimity toward humanity.

AUGUST 26

*Passion is the smoke and emotion is the glow of love's fire;
unselfishness is the flame that illuminates the path.*

Do not blame the ignorant for their vices. Each vice is the shadow of some virtue. The more you blame another for his or her vice, the more you keep that vice-seed in the world where it can feed upon others. By this attention evil is continued in the world. But knowing that vice is nothing but the effect of *nufs* to control energy, one can perceive the hand of God even in wickedness. Find God, discern the good in all tendencies, and you help to purify the universe.

AUGUST 27

The soul of Christ is the light of the universe.

The single expression *Nuri Mohammed* characterizes both the soul of Christ and the light of the universe. This light permeates the cosmos, and it is through it that humanity finds all love, all wisdom, and all joy.

AUGUST 28

Death is a tax the soul has to pay for having had a name and form.

Soul does not die, form dies. Soul does not die, name dies. Life is a journey from aeon to aeon and yet is not a journey. Circumstances change, essences never. We don and doff cloaks, which we call bodies, which are not ourselves. Such is the nature of creation.

AUGUST 29

A pure life and a clean conscience are as two wings attached to the soul.

By the pure life is meant a life free from any attachments, a heart filled with love, a mind illuminated by Supreme Thought. The clean conscience is also dependent upon Unity, knowing neither good nor evil, for as soon as action is so divided whatever elevates also creates accommodation for depression and thus deprives the soul of happiness.

AUGUST 30

The giver is greater than the gift.

For giving itself increases the greatness of heart and mind. Whatever one attaches value to, the value is in the attachment not in the thing, and this is a false value. There is nothing in the universe so valuable as that which can be given away yet retained in the giving such as the heart-qualities, which spring from love. All else is valuable only because humanity considers it so.

AUGUST 31

One who has spent has used; one who has collected has lost;
but one who has given has saved his or her treasure forever.

The real treasure is in the heart. What one spends is only an exchanging of values. It is a kind of barter. What one has collected, one becomes guardian of and so slave to. But when one gives away—whether something of matter or intellect or spirit—one has given away that which one is master of, whether it is possessions, knowledge, or love.

September 1

Joy and sorrow both are for each other. If it were not for joy,
sorrow could not be; and if it were not for sorrow,
joy could not be experienced.

The heart from its very nature expands and contracts, grows warmer and colder. After contraction, the very nature of life tends to make it to expand again, and there is sorrow, there is a tightening of processes, a deadness and dullness. Pain accompanies the escape from sorrow, but the end of pain is expansion in the spirit, which surely leads to joy.

At the same time, if one becomes so rapt in joy, if one in such moments becomes attached to the self, the joy in turn will lead to further sorrow. The purpose of spiritual development is to understand the nature of life beneath joy and sorrow and so find peace in every experience regardless of its fruits.

September 2

Self-pity is the cause of all life's grievances.

To relate life to the ego is to destroy the value of life without enhancing the value of ego. Once the process of self-pity is begun, it leads away from beauty and happiness. In beauty there is no extension of self, there is forgetfulness of self and sooner or later surrender of self.

SEPTEMBER 3

How can the unlimited Being be limited?
All that seems limited is in its depth beyond all limitations.

Limitation comes from the examination of mind. Mind by its very nature puts a limit on things. The eye in its measure of space sees only so far to the left and right and only so far in front of the body; from this come the laws of perspective important in mathematics and art. Although the mind can see much further in every direction, still it is limited and subject to laws of perspective from which only the illuminated mind can escape. Existence does not depend upon comprehension by mind, which can only comprehend so far. All essence is beyond conception; search as it may, the mind unaided can never find the thing-in-itself.

SEPTEMBER 4

Pleasure blocks, but pain clears the way of inspiration.

Pleasure attaches value to limitations, to names and forms and personalities, while inspiration depends upon the efflux of the Divine Spirit—in other words, *Ishk*. Pleasure always enhances the ego, and as pain restrains the *nufs*, it opens up the greatest possibilities for spiritual development.

SEPTEMBER 5

There is no source of happiness other than that in the human heart.

All material and mental things are subject to growth, change, and decay. Their nature is transitory and their effects evanescent. That joy which is the joy of the moment is no joy for it is limited. The joy of the *Zakir*, the one who is flowing in the divine remembrance, is not restricted by time, space, or condition. It flows out of the center of Being, and its getting and giving are one.

September 6

Happy is one who does good to others;
miserable is one who expects good from others.

When the heart acts, it touches everything in the universe. When a heart feeds another it feeds itself, for it knows no limitation of self. The heart in its true condition expands and gives love and as it gives it receives. But one who expects to be fed by the heart of another has their own heart closed, and as their heart is closed, neither can they receive substance from another. The substance is in the very sphere, and its giving and getting are one.

September 7

One virtue is more powerful than a thousand vices.

The real secret of virtue is strength, is life. Vice is weakness; vice shows the absence of strength and of life. Virtue is born of the true self, vice is the offspring of *nufs*; this is the only standard for measuring vice and virtue. Although humankind often selects particular moral and legislative codes, these are only scientific and sure insofar as they harmonize with those highly spiritual codes given by Moses, Rama, and the other great lawgivers. There is no great virtue in praising law and there is no great sin in breaking law; the merit comes from understanding law, while lack of understanding keeps one back on one's journey.

September 8

The soul is either raised or cast down by the
power of its own thought, speech, and action.

Thought, speech, and action are all movements. All depend upon the breath, upon the rising and falling of the life currents which affect the personality through the breath. When there is no thought there is no movement in the ordinary sense, and as the soul is non-spatial it cannot then be raised up or cast down. It is only when acts, words, and thoughts harmonize—either with the upward or downward movements of the breath (*Urouj* and *Nasoul*)—that the soul is raised up or cast down. But when the breath is balanced in the *Kemal* state the effect is totally different.

SEPTEMBER 9

Love is the divine Mother's arms;
when those arms are spread, every soul falls into them.

Although the word "fall" is used here, the action is of the contrary nature. That is to say, there is a movement upward, at least in the sense that one is raised above the mind-mesh and freed from the turmoil and complexities resulting from ordinary thought and action. This love is the very essence of the soul and it is the life that makes a soul realize its true nature.

SEPTEMBER 10

It is the fruit that makes the tree bow low.

True humility is characteristic of the wise one who knows, who has gathered the harvest. The proud one has to hold up his or her head; it stands not by itself. But the wise one, seeing the power there and recognizing that the power is the gift of God, surrenders that gift back to the Giver of all good things.

From another point of view, fruit is a burden, whether that burden takes the form of wealth, knowledge, power, or friends. All of these have a purpose, but when that purpose is out of harmony with one's spiritual unfoldment its burdensome nature becomes manifest.

SEPTEMBER 11

In order to learn forgiveness, one must first learn tolerance.

This is true whether one offers forgiveness or begs forgiveness. To offer forgiveness without having understanding is no real forgiveness, for it does not absolve another from the sin, and it does not free another from Karma. The real forgiveness—as exemplified in the lives of Christ and Mohammed—is to give something to the one who has gone astray, to impart life and love and lesson so that one will not err again. The average so-called forgiveness which does not deter another from erring again has no value.

Likewise, begging forgiveness is of no value unless there be repentance. If you are unwilling to repent, there is no gain and there may be a decided loss in begging pardon. Sufis have always placed considerable importance upon repentance, comparatively little upon forgiveness.

SEPTEMBER 12

The first step toward forgiveness is to forget.

That is to say, remove all remembrance of the act from the mind. The one who has done wrong does this best by a complete change of attitude, so great a change that the mind will not again succumb to a similar temptation, will not permit the ego to sway it in the wrong direction. Those who have been wronged should steel themselves against being wronged again. In the first stage, one completely erases all recollection from the mind or ceases to regard the deed as an evil one—especially if one has learned a living lesson through the experience. This prepares one for the higher condition which is not to be insulted, not be wronged or hurt by another. This shows real spiritual advancement on the part of a person, that he or she is not affected or harmed by the acts, thoughts, or words of another.

SEPTEMBER 13

The only way to live in the midst of inharmonious influences is to strengthen the will power and endure all things, yet keeping fineness of character and nobility of manner together with an ever-living heart full of love.

There are two ways to reach and hold this stage. One is through *Darood*—to hold tight to the Divine Thought on the breath. Keep unbroken concentration no matter what the occurrence or cause for complaint. Stay focused, and concentrate all the thought upon Allah so that nothing another says, does, or thinks can affect the mind. Then the mind is protected and the karmic reaction strikes the other.

At the same time, the heart should be kept pure for even the thought of another as other, even the idea of dualism with favorable opinions is not conducive to the spiritual welfare of any party concerned. Heart full of love is heart that does not conceive differences, which holds another as the self, which feels all people as the offspring of the one Divine Parent.

SEPTEMBER 14

Devotion to a spiritual teacher is not for the sake of the teacher; it is for God.

By attunement to the breath of the spiritual teacher, one becomes attuned to the Divine Breath, and by attunement to the heart of the teacher one becomes united to all the illuminated souls who form the Embodiment of the Master, the Spirit of Guidance.

SEPTEMBER 15

To become cold from the coldness of the world is weakness;
to become broken by the hardness of the world is feebleness;
but to live in the world and yet to keep above it is like walking on the water.

This is the very test of life and it affects mankind on all planes. Thus in the physical body, when we are losers in the battle of life, whether through our own weakness in the economic field or because of heedlessness, often this takes the form of cold in the extremities. This is due to poor circulation, which in turn is the result of lack of life-force in the heart.

The struggle for life is a battle and very often those who are unwilling to fight others are likewise unwilling to overcome their own weaknesses. This shows absence of life and power. The purpose of the purification of heart is in the highest degree scientific when viewed from this aspect, as the soul through the heart replenishes the energy in all of one's vehicles down to the utmost cell.

From the emotional point of view, the order and rhythm of the circulation is necessary to maintain health and vigor, and also in order that one not be overcome through external forces. In meeting the struggles of existence, a bold posture is put on through concentration on the heart. This boldness is inner not outer; it is a fine courage which may be hidden by meekness and a true humility. It knows no fear, yet it disdains neither anger nor egotism. This shows the control of heart and will over mind.

And the mind, thus handled, may keep its opinions or change them. But mind is not opinion. Opinion is a fixation of mind due to the *nufs*. Opinions are like hardening and sculpturing mind-stuff into images and then worshiping the images. This is a kind of idolatry. Mind freed from opinion is the master-mind. In this the water element is symbolic of the mind-stuff (or *akasha*), which rises and falls but never sweeps over the head of the one who has mastery.

SEPTEMBER 16

God alone deserves all love, and the freedom of love is in giving it to God.

The idea of "I love" or "she loves" is good but not complete. Until it is complete, life is not complete. Possession in love is desecration of love; there is no property in love, there is surrender in love. Yet this very surrender is no loss; one becomes like a magnet which imparts its magnetism to all things yet loses no power thereby. So the freedom and surrender come together.

SEPTEMBER 17

Love has the power to open the door of eternal life.

Because love is life—they are not two, they are one. The only force in animal passion is the life-force, and this life-force leads to propagation of species. The transmutation of love from the sphere of procreation to creation is a transmutation of life-force, which may then be directed at will. Yet all our usages of this life-force should be for the greatest satisfaction possible in order that beauty may increase and every deed become a work of art.

When one reaches this stage, one brings paradise to earth and one lives one's immortality. Immortality, being of the nature of the infinite, is therefore unqualified and knows no self. The true *Atman*, if the totality can so be called, is life, but life not in the sense that it is generally known. Rather it is *Ishk*, the Supreme Love which bonds everything in creation and yet is bound by nothing.

September 18

Love has its limitations when it is directed towards limited beings,
but love directed to God has no limitations.

Directed love is like focused light. If even a little of the light of the sun is focused it starts a fire, as can be witnessed by the use of the sunglass. Therefore, while passion has power it is lacking in beauty and destroys either the object of passion or the one manifesting it. In love, power and beauty are in equilibrium and remain so until one is covered by the other.

In true love, whatever its plane, power and beauty are balanced, and such love brings joy although it is not sought for the sake of joy. It is life itself, and when that love, that life, and that beauty are spread out to the Omniscient God, it brings God into our being and we are, as the Bible says, gods indeed.

September 19

The teacher, however great, can never give his or her knowledge to the pupil;
the pupil must create his or her own knowledge.

Knowledge and life are not separate. This is the meaning of the *Ilm* of the Sufis which is not like the knowledge of the world. Naming is not knowledge, hearing is not knowledge, and reading is not knowledge. Experience is knowledge. Life brings knowledge, and the removal of self enables one to find knowledge in everything.

All the teacher can do is to make the pupil realize this, but the knowledge of the pupil is that of the pupil's own realization. That is why it is difficult for the average person to study with understanding the lives and precepts of the great teachers of humanity.

SEPTEMBER 20

*One thing is true: although the teacher cannot give the knowledge,
the teacher can kindle the light if the oil is in the lamp.*

This oil is love, and the lamp is the heart. Once the flame even flickers a bit, it starts a commotion and a motion which reaches to the furthest parts of one's being. Often this occurs in sorrow or in trepidation, yet it awakens the life-spark in one to the real life. Thus this awakening comes with sympathy and understanding. If one then keeps in the rhythm of the heart and watches the heart fully, all things become clear in the light and life of the heart, and that very attitude fans the flame therein to greater brightness.

SEPTEMBER 21

**Will power is the keynote of mastery,
and asceticism is the development of will power.**

This will-power is both love-power and life-power. When it expresses itself as power it is called "will." That is to say, in love—true love—power, intelligence, and beauty should be in equilibrium. When beauty dominates there is adoration which leads to intoxication, and when power dominates there is more fire without always more light.

In order that will-power be not destructive, in order that it be one with intelligence and beauty, the spiritual life is followed, which concentrates everything upon Unity. No doubt the life of self-denial in the desert accomplishes it, but that is like spending all one's time gathering fuel for a fire, which is used neither to cook food nor to warm others. The real spiritual asceticism is followed in the midst of the world. This is nothing but a willing surrender for the purpose of a greater benefit for oneself and the whole humanity.

SEPTEMBER 22

Real generosity is an unfailing sign of spirituality.

Real generosity shows the absence of the sway of the *nufs*. To give freely means to give without attaching any value to giver, giving, or gift.

SEPTEMBER 23

*There are two kinds of generosity; the real and the shadow;
the former is prompted by love, the latter by vanity.*

Often it is hard to draw a line between them for even among the vain there is often a spark of love. For instance, even those who give selfishly are not so bad as the misers who give not at all. The miser will have to learn to give as well as to find joy in giving, so for the miser there is a long road. But the other one who has practiced giving yet not found joy in it will have less difficulty.

But it is not true generosity which imparts things with the thought of self in them. What is known as "Indian giver" is one who recalls gifts, but the vain person is often a spiritual Indian giver who repeats, "Remember I gave you that thing." In such giving there is no life and consequently no blessing.

For this reason, many who practice healing, who possess some psychic power, do not do real spiritual healing. They give out some magnetism, no doubt, but the real substance of life is seldom transmitted in that way. This often leads to but temporary relief as well as added danger to the one practicing the art. The true healing is healing from the *nufs*, the cause of all diseases.

SEPTEMBER 24

*It is better to pay than to receive from the vain;
for such favors demand ten times their cost.*

All praise is due to God. Wishing thanks or appreciation for self is nothing but idolatry and often a most vicious form of idolatry. Sufis do not attack those who worship sticks and stones, but evil are they who, though they enter a thousand temples or churches, demand for themselves what belongs to Allah alone.

SEPTEMBER 25

The kingdom of heaven is in the hearts of those who realize God.

For only such possess all powers, faculties, and gifts—yet in doing so they possess nothing. Possessions are burdens that impede progress. Possessions are blocks that prevent the free flow of energy, hindering the electricity of life from flowing freely through the veins of nature. There can be no pretense here, neither the desire to give nor to receive. Freedom is necessary and freedom is impossible when one is not free from thoughts.

The master of thought does not "think" in the ordinary sense of the term, nor does he or she love in the ordinary sense. What thought may come through one, what love may pass through one, is the natural concomitant of one's life and realization. Of this it is impossible to say much in words.

SEPTEMBER 26

In order to relieve the hunger of others we must forget our own hunger.

First, considering physical want: food or clothing should be given with a blessing, with a feeling that imparts life to another. The mere presentation of something without this feeling may turn a gift into a curse, for every particle of such food may bring life or disease. Only by removing the idea of self from our action of giving can we be sure that it will bring life.

The same principle applies when one considers the knowledge to be given to another, even the knowledge of the world. You cannot teach geography, arithmetic, language, or anything to another if you put self into the picture. Self does not belong there. And so when it comes to satisfying the hunger of the heart, we feed others either with our personal food or with that drawn from the universe. If we give this heart-food for the sake of getting, poison is transferred and hunger may be followed by death. But if in the giving we consider it our duty—whether spiritual or ethical duty— then someone benefits and perhaps all concerned benefit.

September 27

It is when you have lost the idea of separateness and feel yourself at one with all creation that your eyes are opened and you see the cause of all things.

This is the union of feeling and knowledge. As Krishna has so beautifully expressed it, "To those ever attached to Me, worshiping Me in love, I give that union to knowledge by which they come to Me." Such universal expression alone is valuable. Separating self from self, we place boundary marks upon knowledge and so make omniscience impossible. People speak about higher mind and completeness of mind. There can be no such completeness without love. Even if love takes that cool form called interest it is something, for without that interest there would be no knowledge. And what is interest? It is a turning and a tuning—a turning and a tuning often quite similar to the process by which one attains to any or every goal sought.

September 28

To fall beneath one's ideal is to lose one's share of life.

That is to say, since the ideal is the highest of concepts, the whole of the vital force for which one has capacity cannot be expressed or felt unless act, speech, and thought are in harmony with it. The practice of *tasawwuri Murshid,* practicing oneness with your teacher, as well as the practice of *Darood* by Sufis make it possible to retain some relationship, even identity, with the ideal at all times. Average people, not knowing these principles, often have no means by which they can maintain their state, so they rise and fall and are subject to both joy and sorrow.

Actually life is expressed through the ideal, the ideal in this event being higher than the idea. Idea is a thought which is connected with *nufs*; ideal, while not always free from *nufs*, is in the direction of independence from *nufs*. To attain to any ideal, no matter what its characteristics, one must remove the *nufs* from one's path. Therefore, selfishness is a bar even to passion, crime, and aggrandizement. Fortunately the wicked people do not generally know this so they are caught by their own misdeeds.

SEPTEMBER 29

The wise of all ages have taught that it is knowledge of
the divine Being that is life, and the only reality.

That is to say, *Ilm* is knowledge and knowledge is nothing but *Ilm*. Worldly knowledge is symbolical—the application of names to processes. But understanding of the processes requires a subtle union with them. Naming a thing does not bring knowledge of it. One can distinguish electricity from magnetism and light, but what is electricity? What is magnetism? What is light? We know only so far as our senses tell us or as far as our limited mind has opportunity to convey some idea.

Yet from a certain point of view, there is a great reality in electricity, in magnetism, and in light beyond their phenomenal appearance and even beyond nominal conception. There is a reality that can be experienced in *Zikr*, where the three are one. A person will then know, without always being able to explain, that electricity, magnetism, and light are certain aspects of life which appear more clearly when seen in the mineral (or chemical) world. They are present in vital processes, though more hidden. And when we come to humanity we observe other forms of magnetic behavior closely interwoven with the personality. This shows that true magnetism is connected with life.

Above and beyond the sphere of mind is *Ishk*, the Universal Subtle Energy which is what we call Love. Comprehension of *Ishk* is *Ilm*, but neither *Ishk* nor *Ilm* is possible without union with the Supreme Being, at least in the form included in *Darood*. That union is still possible in name and form, for *Baqa*, or awakening to the real self, is the goal of all. That is to say, the expression of the Divine Light and Love awakens in and through our personalities. This brings all knowledge and all gifts.

SEPTEMBER 30

When the stream of love flows in its full strength, it purifies all that stands in its way, as the Ganges, according to the teaching of the ancients, purifies all those who plunge into its sacred waters.

The real Ganges, the real Jordan, the real Red Sea is the human heart and its tributaries. Heart heals body, heart heals mind, heart heals heart, heart heals all that pertains to the self, and heart heals all that pertains to others (that is to say to the phenomenal non-self). Heart takes one above the realm of self and non-self. Heart is the throne of Unity.

All the teaching of Sufism is to bring one to this great realization of Heart. This secret is described in Hazrat Inayat Khan's text "Nirtan," but not revealed. It cannot be revealed if by revelation one means making clear some mystery for the head. It will always be a mystery to the mind; it need never be a mystery to the heart.

This realization is the most important thing in life, in the highest sense. It is the eternal life which is possible whenever one lays down the ego and surrenders gladly. Without that surrender there is no plunge into the Ganges, there is no division of the Red Sea or baptism in the Jordan. This supreme Unity is above mind, beyond the mind-mesh. In that realm, *Bhakti* and *Jnana*—union through love and through knowledge—become one.

OCTOBER 1

Each soul's attainment is according to its evolution.

That is to say, the soul sees life openly insofar as it is uncovered and no longer veiled by its vehicles. Removal of matter, removal of mind, removal of heart—these are the three stages in the evolution (so-called) of soul.

OCTOBER 2

It always means that you must sacrifice something very dear to you when God's call comes.

This includes sacrifice of all things, but as even the most selfish person does not attach value to "all things," one only feels the sacrifice of what one has valued. What is valued might be wealth, but the wealthy one may be quite willing to surrender worldly knowledge; it might be worldly knowledge, but the learned one may be quite willing to surrender his or her friends; it might be friendship, yet the philanthropist may be willing to sacrifice everything else. Yet hand, head, and heart—in clinging— prevent one from accepting the Divine Grace freely given to all.

OCTOBER 3

Renunciation is always for a purpose;
it is to kindle the soul that nothing may hold it back from God;
but when it is kindled, the life of renunciation is not necessary.

Now renunciation is a letting go of things, but this does not make things depart. One can surrender the title to one's home, yet live in it. It is this kind of surrender which is important in the spiritual life. The Bible teaches, "The earth is the Lord's and the fullness thereof." What is meant by this fullness? It signifies that every blessing that comes to one while on earth comes from God.

OCTOBER 4

There are those who are like a lighted candle:
they can light other candles but the other candles must be of wax;
if they are of steel, they cannot be lighted.

Buzurg is one who can kindle the hearts of others even without speech; his or her personality alone may be able to accomplish this. Everyone is a potential *Buzurg*, which is to say, *Bodhisattva*—the essential nature of the Sufi *Buzurg* being the same as that of the Buddhist *Bodhisattva*. Such a one is an instrument of the Spirit of Guidance, the incarnate spirit of the Divine Master.

Buzurg can affect most everybody, but in two ways. Some are like the wax candle, that once the heart is kindled it is always kindled. It may require some effort to light it, but once the flame appears the rest is sure. In these there is the fire of love. But others are like the piece of iron or steel which is magnetized in the presence of some force but does not retain its magnetism. Often these souls appear brilliant, even highly inspired in the presence of *Buzurg*, but elsewhere and otherwise they are no different from ordinary people.

The really hard-hearted ones have as much fire, as much energy, even as much love as others, but their direction in life is wrong; they become attached to this wrong direction and in the end lose all hope and all permanent success.

OCTOBER 5

There is no greater scripture than nature, for nature is life itself.

Nature is both the forms we see and the essence permeating those forms. Without that life the forms would express neither beauty nor inspiration, for illumination of mind depends upon the kindling of both its thoughts and essence. Nature is more than the forms and yet dependent on forms. God created the world as a mirror to God's Self, and the beauty of that mirror of Nature is the beauty of God. In that mirror of Nature, in other words of life, we can study the reflection of God.

OCTOBER 6

Wisdom can only be learned gradually, and every soul is not ready to receive or to understand the complexity of the purpose of life.

By "soul" here, really "mind" is meant. Mind learns by a series of steps and stages, while heart learns at a single glance. Thus while some teach evolution and others revolution, while some teach gradual progress and others propound suddenness, there is truth in both. In the case of gradual progress soul is identified with mind, in the case of suddenness of realization with heart. Actually soul is neither mind nor heart, but in speaking of wisdom we refer to those vehicles. Wisdom is life itself reflected in the individual being.

OCTOBER 7

It is a very high stage on the path of love when one really learns to love another with a love that asks no return.

This is the real condition on the path of love: that one gives out love and asks no return. So long as one expects love from another creature, of whatever degree, that is reflected love. It is only in God and from God that giving and receiving are one and the same. Heart feeds heart and nothing else feeds heart. Heart can feed heart of self, and it can feed mind of self, and body of self. Heart can also feed the heart of another, mind of another, and body of another. All healing, all help, all love come from heart, which is to say, they come from God, Who is hidden in the heart of each and every person.

October 8

Love alone is the fountain from which all virtues fall as drops of sparkling water.

Virtue is life itself as reflected in the human moral nature. By moral nature is meant that which gives qualities to life, speech, thought, and action. This moral nature is connected with essence of mind, and this essence of mind (*Citta*) really belongs to heart.

Every virtue is an outpouring of life—that is to say, of *Ishk* as *Ishk* touches the surface of life. In the depths it is *Ishk*; on the surface it becomes the various moral qualities, or as Shakespeare has beautifully put it, "The quality of mercy is not strained, it droppeth as the gentle rain from heaven."

October 9

The whole purpose of life is to make God a reality.

Now life is nothing but God, and God's purpose in the creation is to know God's own Self and love God's own Self and express God's own Self. This is the supreme purpose and the essence of purpose: it is the seed of the purpose of every individual entity taking form on any plane.

October 10

If you seek the good in every soul, you will always find it,
for God is in all things; still more, God is in all beings.

The "thingness" in things is that which holds the particles together into a unity. And what is this? It is cohesion, in other words, love. And what is it that keeps beings as beings? It is also a form of cohesion which, while sometimes called life, is really *Ishk*. Without *Ishk* there could be no form, no entities—not even thoughts—for there would be no coherence, only Chaos. And what is *Ishk*? It is the essential quality which characterizes the personality of God, so that God is not only emptiness but also absolute fullness.

OCTOBER 11

The knowledge of God is beyond humanity's reason;
the secret of God is hidden in the knowledge of unity.

The knowledge of God precedes illumination of mind and causes it. It is not strictly speaking acquired by any accumulative method. In this sense, there is no evolution. Yet there is evolution in the sense that as the heart awakens the mind does grow. Illumination of mind is the result of knowledge of God, not the cause of it. Therefore both mystics and scholars have practiced meditation.

To the mystic, meditation means the centering of all the consciousness on Supreme Deity, the nature or characteristic of which is definite. That is to say, God is love, mercy, and all the attributes, and while knowledge of the attributes is not knowledge of God, attainment of the Supreme includes such knowledge. That is to say, *Ilm* or supreme knowledge includes *Hakma* or universal science.

Now scholars, while they do not always recognize heart as the center of the intuitive faculty, often find it advantageous to clear their mind of all concepts—not only of false concepts but of all concepts—to facilitate the mind's operation. Therefore scholars can often be raised to a higher degree through their own processes. This is the way of *Jnana Yoga*, or union with God through knowledge.

Sufis include all systems in their sciences and regard the Divine Knowledge not as the only valuable knowledge but as the **only** knowledge. In other words, all knowledge is knowledge of God, but many people do not know it.

OCTOBER 12

Seek God in all souls, good or bad, wise or foolish,
attractive and unattractive; in the depths of each there is God.

Since God is the only being, God is the essence and life of all souls. To confuse the soul with the *nufs* of personality is to draw confusion to one's own mind. If there were not some good in the personality, the mind and body could not function. Evil is weakness, and goodness is strength—even the strength that holds body together as a unit or mind together as a unit. The cause of suicide is weakness, and murderers are often suicides who objectify their own weakness. Unable to dominate themselves they desire to dominate others.

The Bowl of Saki Commentary 159

The way to overcome this weakness in others is to practice the spiritual breaths in their presence and so build up the atmosphere. The more positive one is in the presence of such people, the more respect is gained and so everybody can be helped. It is not necessary to judge: the stone is a stone, the tree is a tree, the bird is a bird, but the life in all is God.

OCTOBER 13

When in ourselves there is inharmony, how can we spread harmony?

The best way to develop strength is to achieve unity. This comes out of the practice of concentration. Concentration need not be limited to a few minutes a day or week when one performs some exercise given in the teachings. Concentration may be practiced every hour, every minute, every breath— especially through *Darood*. Then one does not have to seek unity, unity will seek one.

When added to that the *talib* is given instruction in music or else in meditation, he or she acquires that unity of purpose, that unity of feeling, and the more they adhere to that unity the better they can protect themselves and assist others. Never surrender to anything, to anyone, to any force except God or those who represent God in the Spiritual Hierarchy.

OCTOBER 14

The innermost being of a human is the real being of God.

God is in the heart, but God is not the heart. Heart is an accommodation; it is an attunement through a selection exercised in the Supreme whereby, evoking a certain note, a center of consciousness makes itself felt. This center comes out of love and knows nothing but love, and its love is its knowledge and its love commands all knowledge. This heart is not the same as other hearts, but neither is it different. All hearts form God, yet God is not conditioned by them. The light is everywhere, yet by covering itself, so to speak, it forms innumerable lamps—the light of which resembles a tremendous, incomparable harmony.

OCTOBER 15

Love itself is the healing power and the remedy for all pain.

Pain manifests through mind, and pain is only possible when *nufs* holds sway. When a hand is cut, a unity has been broken; when the natural movements of the body have been obstructed, a unity is broken. Every pain shows absence of unity, and love shows presence of unity. In unity is all strength. Pain is only possible when breath does not reach a part. But breath cannot force itself to any area of the body or mind; it must be directed by will, which is nothing but heart.

OCTOBER 16

By loving, forgiving, and serving, it is possible for your whole life
to become one single vision of the sublime beauty of God.

This is because within these processes there is no *nufs*, no shadow. The absence of these processes causes shadow or is caused by shadow; their presence causes the shadows of life to vanish, all common pain and suffering to go. The supreme vision cannot be forced, but neither can it be kept away when one has laid aside all accumulation of selfhood. It becomes the most natural thing in life because it is life itself.

OCTOBER 17

Mysticism to the mystic is both science and religion.

In Sufic terms, there is no difference between *Tasawwuf* and *Ilm*. That is to say, metaphysics, knowledge, mysticism, science, and religion are all one and the same thing to the inner person. The mind may give different names to its different processes, but in the sphere of the heart there is an eternal grasping which can be called love, will, or intuition. These are but names of the same process according to the method by which it influences mind.

When one considers that all love springs from God, all knowledge springs from God, all being is God, how can there be any difference between science, religion, and mysticism? In the realm of duality, in the region of universal becoming, there seems to be differences, but in the sphere of principle, there is not. Real science is comprehension, which is only possible when the heart is awake. Real religion is knowledge of God. Mysticism is the philosophy that God can be known, discovered in the heart of the human being.

OCTOBER 18

The principles of mysticism rise from the human heart;
they are learnt by intuition and proved by reason.

The fundamentality of the heart is proved, proved by the direct experiences of the inner life. Once this is attained, the value of reason becomes evident. Although reason is of little value after the goal is achieved, there is nothing without value. We can argue for reason, we can argue against reason, we can argue with reason, we can even argue in a most irrational manner. All these mean little; but after one has the knowledge one can express it in a most reasonable manner. In other words, reason—which to the average person is a sword and not a shield—to the mystic is a shield first.

OCTOBER 19

Your work in life must be your religion, whatever your occupation may be.

In other words, your work in life is your *Dharma*. This is the purpose of every person's life, for which purpose they sojourn on the earth plane. To divide part of life—dedicating some to God, some to self, some to family or friends—is to misconstrue the purpose of life, which is to seek first that *Dharmic* purpose and not to divide at all.

There is a great deal of difference between piety and real religion. Piety considers self and God. True religion does not consider self. Even unbelievers who are free from heedlessness and thoughtlessness are on the way to the goal, though they walk backwards or with their eyes closed. By the practice of *Darood*, a person practices religion at all times.

OCTOBER 20

*The true joy of every soul is in the realization of the divine Spirit,
and the absence of realization keeps the soul in despair.*

Joy of body comes chiefly from purely physical pleasures, yet in them there is almost always satisfaction of mind. Satisfaction of mind is dependent upon time and space and is not separate from dissatisfaction of mind. That is to say, there are moments when one condition predominates; there are other moments when there is the other condition. Besides that, satisfaction of mind and body depend considerably upon what is outside of body and mind.

Inner satisfaction is not based upon any such flimsy foundation. Soul is either awake or asleep, and its wakefulness is joy and nothing but joy. The states of the heart wherein it feels presence or absence affect the whole personality. Sufis practice *Zikr* and contemplation whereby consciousness enters into union with the Supreme. This is the joy, the intoxication of soul, the drinking of the Divine Wine.

OCTOBER 21

*Beyond the narrow barriers of race and creed we can all unite,
because we all belong to one God.*

Race, creed, and all barriers are productions of one's mind. While it is true historically that there are divisions of humanity, and it is true that geographically all people cannot be in the same place, yet the real barrier is mental, which says, "I am different and you are different." What is this difference? It is what is perceived or conceived. Beyond conception and perception where there is love, there are no such distinctions.

All people were born in a similar manner. The bodies and minds of humanity have the same composition. Emotions are caused according to the same principles. And all are subject to the same laws. Where then do these lines of demarcation arise? It is from lack of knowledge and selfishness on one's part; they do not belong to reality.

OCTOBER 22

All forms of worship or prayer draw one closer to God.

Because they lead away from selfness, they proclaim some ideal, and no matter what that state or condition, no matter what the form, meekness—or being "poor in spirit" as Jesus says—always removes obstacles from one's path. Thus real prayer gives strength, by removing the weakness in one's own nature, which is the greatest bar to success.

OCTOBER 23

When one is separated from God in one's thought,
one's belief is of no use, one's worship is of little use.

Just as in electricity there must be a circuit that current may flow, so in the divine life on a much greater scale must there be a circuit. By cutting God asunder, by making God in one's mind as something different, something apart, there can be no worship, there can be no love. Love unites, and the worship of a tree or flower may contain more of divinity than the prayer wherein God is placed far away. If God is love, if God is like Father or Mother, how can God be far away?

OCTOBER 24

The source of the realization of truth is within one;
one's self is the object of one's realization.

Otherness and ignorance are the same. Sight is in the eye, thought is in the mind, feeling is in the heart. Without sight one could not perceive, without mind one could not conceive, without heart one could not achieve. Success consists of finding the true purpose of body, mind, and heart. It does not consist in dominating anything outside yourself, although this may naturally follow because of the laws of attunement and correspondences. But the supreme satisfaction, the supreme success, the only lasting victory is to find what we are, to know what we are.

OCTOBER 25

True self-denial is losing one's self in God.

This is not to say "I am" or "I am not," it is to give no thoughts to self but all to God. Let one say, "What would God have me say, what would God have me think, what would God have me do?" But even this is unnecessary for there is always a feeling of ease if not of joy, when one practices *Darood*—to harmonize all action, speech, and thought with the breath. This is easy, simple, and sufficient, and for it no knowledge of metaphysics is necessary.

OCTOBER 26

It is more important to find out the truth about one's self,
than to find out the truth of heaven and hell.

What are Heaven and Hell? They are the results of action, speech, and thought—they are "results" and not self-dependent. Every Hell and Heaven may be different, and the same condition can be Hell to one and Heaven to another. Therefore we cannot understand them until we understand self—and not *nufs* but the innermost being.

Sufis willingly surrender Heaven and Hell to God, considering it a joy when Allah is present even in the midst of Hell and a loss when Allah is absent even in the bosom of Paradise.

OCTOBER 27

According to one's evolution, one knows the truth;
and the more one knows, the more one finds there is to know.

Truth stands above and beyond all facts. Truth is the comprehension of life itself, of God. There is no end to such knowledge, which is called the Supreme Knowledge. Therefore it cannot be explained in words or thoughts. Only the illuminated mind can sense it and mind cannot illuminate itself. Just as the light of the moon is drawn from the sun, reflected in the moon, so the light of the mind is drawn from the heart, reflected in mind. Sufis cultivate heart, which means to live by feeling, keeping in harmony with God, and this is possible according to the prescriptions given to each one by Murshid, or by Murshid's representative.

OCTOBER 28

One filled with the knowledge of names and forms has no capacity for the knowledge of truth.

Mind is Heaven and Hell. The *akasha* or accommodation is not so different from the sky. We see sky at day or night: in the day there is a single torch—the Sun—yet all illumination; in the night there are many lamps—the Stars—yet darkness. Sky at night is like the mind replete with knowledge of names and forms—it is still in darkness, while sky at day is like illuminated mind.

These two aspects have been called astral and Buddhic, which are not so much conditions of mind but conditions related to mind. The astral world is the result of mind divided, and it is impossible for Sufis to be contained here, as they practice *Darood* and thus escape all delusion and all snares. The Buddhic condition indicates heart and mind coordinated making truth possible. Therefore Buddha has sometimes been regarded as a solar deity. This is true insofar as mind is concerned, but it is equally true with respect to everyone of the rank of *Rassoul*.

Higher than this is the condition where there is neither day nor night.

OCTOBER 29

One is mistaken when one begins to cultivate the heart by wanting to sow the seed oneself, instead of leaving the sowing to God.

Every form of attachment to self tends to keep the heart closed no matter how great the desire. Even attachment to heart cannot open heart. No desire, no ambition, no hope can do it. It comes from surrender of self and then heart opens almost automatically. Either we are at the helm, or the Spirit of Guidance leads us on.

OCTOBER 30

We start our lives as teachers, and it is very hard for us to learn to become pupils. There are many whose only difficulty in life is that they are teachers already. What we have to learn is pupilship. There is but one teacher, God.

Teacher is the positive pole, and gives; pupil is the negative pole, and takes. Many want to take and also want to teach at the same time; this is impossible and leads to much misery. One is not teacher who seeks followers; one is a seeker of followers. One is only a teacher who teaches others something, who gives others something. It is not necessary to teach, it is not necessary to give. This condition is associated with *Nasoul*, or the rising energy.

Nasoul has its purpose and *Urouj*, the descending energy, has its purpose. There must be balance and order in the Universe. No doubt *Urouj* leads to selfishness, but *Urouj* also leads to growth; merely to give away for the sake of giving is of no great advantage. This assumes that self has capacity for endless evolution. Such self has not the capacity.

It is God Who is, and our evolution is God's evolution; God's opportunity is our opportunity. Therefore *Urouj* and *Nasoul* balance, and when we are willing to learn, God is there to teach us.

OCTOBER 31

Earthly knowledge is as clouds dimming the sight, and it is the breaking of these clouds—in other words, purity of heart—that gives the capacity for the knowledge of God to rise.

"Sight" is more powerful than the eyesight and subtler than the mind. This Sight is insight, which is to say, the sight of the soul independent of its vehicles. In the sphere of matter, it is necessary to become accustomed to a light more dim, the very dimness of which beclouds the mind and keeps it in a sort of haze.

It is oneness of purpose, oneness of character, and the freeing of mind from its subservience to matter that takes it from this hazy condition. Purity of body means body as body, purity of mind means mind as mind, purity of heart means heart as heart. The body has its music and its laws, the mind has its music and its laws, and while heart is greater than any law, it still has its music. Therefore spiritual development is an attunement; yet strange and marvelous to tell, this attunement brings with it all knowledge of all planes.

November 1

Self stands as a wall between human and God.

To use the expressions "greater self" and "lesser self" is unfair unless one has a clear concept of these terms. *Nufs* is not self but is a thought of self that has been given reality as the self. Try to locate *nufs*, concentrate on *nufs*, and often it will be found in a particular part of mind. This shows that *nufs* is a production of mind, not its controller. Then try to locate true self through concentration, and while the force of feeling will be strongest in the heart, centered in the heart, it will touch every portion of one's being. This shows that what humanity ordinarily considers as "I" is not the true "I" and that perhaps there is no true "I." Yes, there is no true "I" except God, of whom the Hebrews said, "I am that I am."

Realizing that the *nufs* is a limitation and not a completeness, one finds the means of circumventing its power—by prayer, meditation, concentration, and all spiritual devotions.

November 2

*It is a patient pursuit to bring water from the depth of the ground;
one has to deal with much mud in digging before one reaches the water of life.*

What is this mud? It is the impure human thought, due from the habit of mind being so dependent upon matter and form. Mind may act independent of all these forms, receiving its knowledge from essence. When the intuitive faculty is aroused, you can know all about the earthly conditions and find it possible to improve these conditions, whether directly connected with yourself or pertaining to the world at large.

Purity of thought means to let God do your thinking, to keep whole-heartedly in devotion to God, which brings all knowledge. So long as you place any value upon your intellect, your memory, your experiences, you cannot reach the highest state. These form the mud and clouds and phantasms of life.

November 3

In one's search for truth, the first lesson and the last is love.
There must be no separation; no "I am" and "Thou art not."
Until one has arrived at that selfless consciousness, one cannot know life and truth.

From the study of the heart in the body, we can observe that it is the circulation of the blood which is the continuous process of life. The blood touches every part of one's body and keeps it functioning as a unit. We can tell something about a person if we know the condition of his or her blood. Heart in the body does not separate part from part but considers the whole as a unit.

Such is the nature of love. It can think only in terms of unities. From one point of view, this is not thinking, but from a deeper aspect it is the only real thinking. What one calls thought—by which one endeavors to know something of the nature of things—is really a process of analysis.

Analysis can only bring knowledge of analyzing; it sees parts but cannot put them together because its nature is to divide. To bring parts together one must be able to efface the *nufs* of each part. By thinking of them as separate pieces one gives each a *nufs*, which is the product of human thought.

In fact, the whole world as we consider its existence is nothing but the external projection of this thought-power, and the physical world itself is dependent upon thought-power to some extent. But thought itself disintegrates when there is not feeling behind it. In fact, this occurs at all times, yet not much attention is paid to it.

As mind analyzes, it cannot put parts together; therefore constantly looking at diversity, it can never apprehend truth. The enlightened mind is not different from the unenlightened mind except that it perceives unity, yet it is not self-dependent, it is dependent upon heart. In fact it is one with heart.

Now heart expands and contracts, but there is no limit to its expansiveness. Whatever it touches, it regards as itself. It sees no separate self and does not think of others as separate. We often find little infants looking upon each other as the same person, calling each other by their own names. They have not yet gained the habit of analyzing and separating. The spiritual soul passes again into a stage when it can see above all the distinctions and differences which divide, when another does not appear to one as another but as a projection of the Self, the Only Being.

This type of love is wisdom itself. When the bounds of limitation are removed, there is no end to wisdom, to knowledge, to ability. However, the real lover does not place the heart upon such things; one loves and it is this love that makes one live. If there are any gains in it, one does not do it for that reason: one loves because it is one's nature to love. This shows the presence of heart which marks the spiritual person. No other person is really spiritual, but all—even sinners—possess this potentiality be it in a smaller or greater degree. Pure thought, real thought, is without any "I" and is the expression of an awakened soul.

NOVEMBER 4

By the power of prayer one opens the door of the heart, in which God, the ever-forgiving, the all-merciful, abides.

Prayer, no matter how selfish it may seem, begins with a petition to a higher power. It admits the limitation of self, and so the Sufi recognizes good in every form of prayer. One also sees the childishness of some forms but regards the devotee as a child rather than as a sinner. In this way God looks upon such prayer. Divine forgiveness is unfathomable for it is God's Nature to forgive. What prevents humanity from receiving this forgiveness is that every sin—in fact every act—makes its mark upon mind. Until one repents, that mark remains on the mind. Repentance is the sign of the awakening of the heart; it is the blood of the penitent which is called the blood of the Lamb in Christian terminology, which removes the thought-mark from the mind.

Sufis call this process "unlearning" when applied to acts or knowledge having no moral quality and "penitence" when applied to acts or knowledge having some moral significance. It is the awakening of heart which removes sins and burdens. Consequently there is no forgiveness without repentance; even God cannot touch the unrepentant until given the opportunity. At least so the Universe operates. While the love of God is beyond analysis, it always produces a maximum of harmony and beauty in life.

November 5

To be really sorry for one's errors is like opening the doors of heaven.

So long as one is unrepentant, thought-marks and thought-shadows mar the mind and prevent beauty from making its appearance. Repentance not only removes these marks and shadows but does the greatest thing possible: it lays the false self low. Thus the poor in spirit are blessed, those devoid of ego attain the gates of Heaven, and only when the mind renounces its possessions can the heart-faculties express themselves in full.

November 6

Our soul is blessed with the impression of the
glory of God whenever we praise God.

Praising God is the real purpose of the Sufi Message. There is no other Message than this: that humanity should lay no stress upon itself and see all values in God. The very nature of soul requires this praise, and its cessation brings all unhappiness. But this praise is not for the sake of happiness although it may bring it; the soul praises because it is its nature to praise.

November 7

As a child learning to walk falls a thousand times before it can stand,
and after that falls again and again until at last it can walk,
so are we as little children before God.

Yes, God is ever ready to receive us. One look at our own hearts, one feeling of sympathy for another, one small prayer, and God, the Divine Father and Mother, takes us in His/Her arms.

November 8

Self-denial is not renouncing things; it is denying the self;
and the first lesson of self-denial is humility.

When the rich young man came to Jesus Christ for advice and was told to sell all that he had and give to the poor, he did not understand the words of the Master. At that time, it was quite common for the rich to come to spiritual teachers and surrender all their worldly goods. This has been a custom through the ages and there is nothing strange in the story—only the European mind, accustomed to different traditions, has not always understood it.

Now anybody is rich in a worldly sense who is intoxicated with life and places values in things—be they riches, possessions, worldly honor, fame, knowledge, or anything which does not lead one to the realization of God. It is almost self-evident that a person cannot serve two masters, be they God and Mammon, or any two masters. The real truth about wealth is that one is never the possessor of such wealth; one is the servant of such wealth. If one possessed it, one could take it with one, both on earthly travels and beyond this plane when one departed. Obviously this is impossible and it teaches that one does not really own things but serves them when one claims such ownership.

Now to renounce what one does not own is not really surrender; to renounce what is one's possession is surrender. The *nufs* is nothing but the thought of self, and this stands in the way of all spiritual realization and perfection. Giving that away, throwing one's sense of self down makes it possible to gain the kingdom of Heaven. The miser on earth, though he or she possesses only a farthing, cannot reach the gates. The kindly person, though he or she have millions, may be blessed by Allah.

November 9

The more elevated the soul, the broader the outlook.

This is both a maxim and a dictum. It is a maxim in the sense that as one progresses in any direction the vision increases. If one travels far physically, the physical vision increases and one becomes more tolerant of people. If one studies much and learns the world's knowledge, it often broadens the mental vision, increases the understanding, and frees one from the toils of time and space.

But if one loves much—or better be it said, if one truly loves—there is no horizon; the whole universe is one's play toy.

Conversely, this is a dictum to the Sufi—to see from all points of view as though one had traveled in every country and understood all speech, habits, and traditions; also to be tolerant and humble as if all worldly knowledge were but an idea of the possible knowledge of humanity. Finally, to know through love that it is love which can give us the widest outlook in life and that there is no limit to that outlook.

November 10

Mastery lies not merely in stilling the mind,
but in directing it towards whatever point you desire.

The first process is to free the mind from influence from outside forces, and the next is to free the will from control by the mind. This is accomplished in meditation. At that point the mind is asleep and needs to be awakened. This is done by the growth of the heart faculties.

What is meant when Hazrat Inayat Khan says "you desire" is that ideal which can be persistently pursued. For this purpose, the Sufis practice concentration. But this deep desire is of the heart and is possible when the will and the heart direct the activities of mind.

We can see these stages in *Zikr*, the first part of which declares, "La Ilaha"—the meaning of which is that there is no divinity in things, in created objects. This part of *Zikr* frees mind from illusion and stills it. The next part of *Zikr*, "El Allahu"—is the positive portion which points directly to God. By it one directs the mind toward the supreme desire and so toward any other beneficial desire.

November 11

Our thoughts have prepared us for the happiness or unhappiness we experience.

The average person under the influence of ego casts shadow thoughts over the heart so that the heart does not experience bliss. Happiness is not to be confused with momentary pleasure. One way to distinguish them is this: any act, speech, or thought which, while bringing some pleasant result, also affects one at some point in an unpleasant manner—that is to say, the result is alloyed—is not of the nature of happiness. A happy condition is one unalloyed, when there is nothing to mar it, when it is one whole, complete, and consistent experience of joy.

By repeating "Toward the One" it is possible to get one complete effect from every cause. This makes possible later, when a happy result is either desirable or given one by Divine Grace, that it is a pure state unaffected by mental shadows or thought forces. Purification of heart helps more than anything else in this direction.

NOVEMBER 12

When the mind and body are restless,
nothing in life can be accomplished. Success is the result of control.

This control is in two parts: first, the practice of *Darood*, including all spiritual exercises by which one voluntarily assumes control over mind and body; second, the activating of heart by which all success and all attainments come to one. This is the positive spiritual life, which is broader than the ordinary life and which is not a negation but a more complete condition.

NOVEMBER 13

When speech is controlled, the eyes speak;
the glance says what words can never say.

If one studies telegraphy, it will be found that the transmitted word or letter is formed by breaks in the current. In other words, energy is transmitted until and unless there is a break, and by these breaks word and letter symbols are formed. The same principle holds true in thought transmission, whether by speech or telepathy. The Divine Energy is always present; speech comes by breaks in the mental magnetism or electricity, by making shadow in the intellectual light. Thus words are formed which convey thoughts.

Pure thought is much deeper and cannot be expressed well in words. Nevertheless, by a flow of spiritual magnetism through the eyes, this purer light flashes out from the inner being. Without word or gesture, when there is attunement between minds and hearts, the thoughts flash back and forward by "makes" and "breaks" in it. This is the same principle as in telegraphy but the vibrations are much more subtle.

November 14

Words are but shells of thoughts and feelings.

For words are conventions which guise thoughts and feelings. Of themselves words are nothing but social arrangements of letters or symbols. It is the thought-force in the word which makes it a living thing. This holds true for things other than words but it is most evident in words which, without that inner essence, are utterly dead.

November 15

Wisdom is not in words, it is in understanding.

As words are caused by breaks in the transmission of energy, they cannot possibly be of the nature of light and they can more certainly be of the nature of shadow. Wisdom is pure light which can flash steadily through the eyes or atmosphere of a personality. It contains all it would convey as a unity which cannot be readily analyzed. Yet it can inspire and strengthen and enable the mind to broaden its horizon.

November 16

The message of God is like a spring of water;
it rises and falls and makes its way by itself.

For the Message of God is destined for humanity. A person is blessed who willingly becomes an instrument of the Message. There is more energy in humanity than in animal, more in animal than in plant, and more in plant than in rock, so the spiritual electricity always tries to flow through the one who offers less resistance to it. When one is unwilling to serve God, the animal or plant or mineral kingdom may take one's place. Sodom and Gomorrah were destroyed by the elements when the people scoffed at the Message, and Palestine flowed with milk and honey when the people listened to God.

November 17

If the eyes and ears are open, the leaves of the trees become as pages of the Bible.

Average people consider their eyes and ears as being open, but really they are practically blind and deaf. For instance, neither can their hearing be compared to that of the blind person nor their sight to that of a deaf one. It is only when one is deprived of the use of the senses that one can realize the value of one of them.

The mystic does not have to be lacking in sense proclivity to learn the value of every part of the body, to see all the Grace with which God has endowed it; neither is the mystic dependent upon the senses. To take full advantage of the capacity of a faculty, it is necessary to coordinate it with the breath and heart. Sufis have many practices by which magnetism can be increased in any part of the body, but the real difficulty is the shadow thrown across the part by the *nufs*.

Most people do not realize that lack of interest falls as a shadow upon the mind and the sense. The mystic, being indifferent, neither increases the interests nor diminishes them but finds in all things a relation to the perfect whole. This prevents the *nufs* from throwing any shadow upon any faculty. There is mysticism in sound and in sight that the seer is cognizant of at all times. By keeping in *Darood* and so letting the Divine Spirit through the breath touch every part of the being, and by concentration in the heart, one brings vitality to every vehicle and every portion of each body. Then one can receive knowledge even from name and form.

November 18

The soul of all is one soul, and the truth is one truth,
under whatever religion it is hidden.

Ishk (or love) unites one to another. One does not regard the fingers as having any reality apart from the body. So the life in us is that which unites us to another. Life is impossible without holding some relation to plant, animal, or human. We are all interdependent, showing that the reality in us is greater than any conception we may hold. Without *Ishk* we would not be.

Yet *Ishk* is force, not personality, and it is not dependent upon personality. That person which is the source of *Ishk* is none other than God or Allah or Brahman or *Dharmakaya*.

This knowledge is vouchsafed to no person so long as that one is considered apart from all others.

NOVEMBER 19

Narrowness is not necessarily devotion but often appears so.

Narrowness is concentration of ego; devotion is concentration of heart. God is not the thought of humanity, and a strong voice or manner does not necessarily mean a strong will. That is to say, one may apply or employ external force yet the result may not be satisfactory. Being out of harmony with Nature, one cannot forever be successful. The devotee, losing his or her self in the ideal, can never make this mistake.

NOVEMBER 20

It is the soul's light which is the natural intelligence.

What is called "*Nur*" is the Universal Light which touches every part of the universe. Without this Light there would be no universe: it is the aspect of *Ishk* which we call Intelligence because it becomes the light of the Mind. Although *Ishk* is all light, it is Oneness. In it there is no Mind, although there is "*Buddhacitta*," the essence of Mind. By an accommodation in the Supreme the light produces forms, but these forms are made out of the vibrations of the light-self. Then the light appears within these forms and enables them to perceive phenomena.

It is, however, the soul which sees, whether through an individual—be that individual rock, plant, animal, human, or planet—or whether it be the sight of body, mind, or heart.

November 21

*The wave is the sea itself; yet, when it rises in the form of a wave,
it is the wave; and when you look at the whole of it, it is the sea.*

Soul, forming a center in the Universal Light, produces heart. In heart soul sees directly, thus producing Universal Intelligence. But as God has produced matter outside the realm of absolute intelligence yet impregnated with Universal Intelligence, the soul—to experience it—must produce a vehicle capable of apprehending it. So the Light-Intelligence is agitated and the waves on its surface produce mind.

Mind being made up of coarser vibrations than heart can look directly upon matter and see it as matter. Heart may perceive matter but would not distinguish matter from spirit because heart does not distinguish. So mind sees all these differences, but when one wishes to look beyond the differences one must see with the heart. When one further wishes to become that which one sees, one enters upon the soul-life. Then sight, seer, and seen are all one.

November 22

It is not the solid wood that can become a flute; it is the empty reed.

From the standpoint of body, body is at its best when it is kept clean from poisons within and contamination without. But the same holds true for mind. We keep on filling the mind with all kinds of thoughts. This does not enlarge mind, rather it puts tremendous weight upon mind. Through meditation mystics clear the mind from all extraneous thoughts until it becomes like a polished mirror. This polished mirror may reflect the light from above or the shadow from below. This is the real use of mind unaffected by self.

Pure mind is the result of the unity of a person within his or her self when the light of the intelligence pouring from and through the heart lightens every part of the being. In Christian terminology, this light is *Logos*, which lightens everyone who has ever come into the world. This makes all genius, all music, and all human intelligence possible.

NOVEMBER 23

Reason is learned from the ever changing world;
but true knowledge comes from the essence of life.

The rational faculty is dependent upon something which is not in and of the mind itself. Either it accepts *a priori* concepts or intuitions or else it produces *a posteriori* conclusions drawn from external observations. The idea of *a priori* conclusions—that is to say, conclusions drawn prior to experience—is good when they are founded upon faith, that is to say, the attunement of heart. But even intuition is of no value unless it is put into practice in life.

So far as the mind depending on the senses, not even the scientists do this. Some philosophers have falsely drawn conclusions by this method, but when philosophers' reasoning is examined, it is generally found that they have assumed *a priori* that conclusions must be *a posteriori*. In other words, it has been something other than reason which has proclaimed the value and supremacy of reason. This is the fallacy and dilemma of all worldly thinkers.

NOVEMBER 24

God is within you; you are God's instrument,
and through you God expresses God's self to the external world.

How is *a priori* reasoning possible? How is *a posteriori* reasoning possible? There must be something beyond mind to do this. If mind is greater than reason, then mind is essence and mind can of itself apprehend all things—then mind is creator and destroyer. In other words, Mind would be God. But since we actually find mind limited and mind learning through reason, reason must be greater than mind.

But what is this reason? It is *Logos*, the Universal Sense. Intuition is not different from reason or antagonistic to it, but it is free from time-processes and also from spatial and egoistic influences. In other words, it gives the answer immediately, but it is the same answer as would come through reason.

This shows that there is something much deeper and more fundamental than mind, which mind cannot conceive but which mind can reflect. This is soul, which is nothing but God. Mind is dependent upon reason and reason upon soul. In other words, God is the true experiencer of all things Who uses the human mind as an observing station. We are only our thought of self, but when our thought is identified with God's thought, one becomes God. Such a one is called a Buddha, sometimes Mahatma.

NOVEMBER 25

It is according to the extent of our consciousness of prayer that our prayer reaches God.

Average people are dependent upon mind, and even though they may be devotees, they cannot pierce the mind-mesh. As soon as one views life from the aspect of the relative non-reality of personality, all life and love enter the prayer. Then prayer becomes *Ishk* and mounts to the throne of God.

NOVEMBER 26

The heart must be empty in order to receive the knowledge of God.

When personality is intrigued by the world it becomes intoxicated by name and form. This produces pleasure and pain. This produces rise and fall and all duality. God is beyond duality, therefore scripture teaches that every valley must be exalted and every mountain brought low. To reach this state, Sufis cultivate indifference—which is really the highest kind of love. When love for one person means not-love for another, then that is passion, not love. The true love, even when thrown upon another will also shine upon everyone, and this is true whether it is thrown upon a personality or upon God.

Human love for human, no matter how great it is, is generally marred by thoughts, which cast shadows upon it. Human love for God, which necessitates ego-sacrifice, permits the light which has always been there to shine through the heart and flood the mind with all knowledge. While it may appear wrong to seek Allah for the sake of knowledge, it is actually impossible to do this, for if one loves knowledge the heart is not empty and so God cannot be the ideal. But when there is no other ideal or love than God, all knowledge and all other desires are attained.

NOVEMBER 27

As long as in love there is "you" and "me," love is not fully kindled.

The spreading of atoms and vibrations causes day. The collection of vibrations into bundles, which is the concentration or contraction of their activity, by drawing more of light into one locality produces shadow in another locality. When shadow is produced, there is no longer universal day.

Likewise in the human concept of love, when one includes oneself in the picture one turns love into my love; when one distinguishes even unconsciously and subtly **my-love** from **my-not-love** or from **love-other-than-my-love**, there is division, and any division betrays absence of love.

NOVEMBER 28

Once you have given up your limited self willingly to the Unlimited,
you will rejoice so much in that consciousness
that you will not care to be small again.

When this is understood, really understood, all smallness will disappear; there will be no war nor pain nor suffering. It is the idea of self—any idea that we attach to our mind—which stabs the very essence of mind and begins that process from which all sorrow arises. Voluntary surrender of self does not destroy mind, does not harm body, and does not annihilate self. Rather it annihilates that thought of self which is given erroneously the name of self.

No one can pretend to the cosmic state. Thought of Sufism or of being a Sufi—even of submitting to the disciplines and practices—does not make one a Sufi. Attainment and only attainment makes one a Sufi. It is wrong ever to call oneself a Sufi, but there are such souls who have lost all consciousness and feeling of distinction and separation, and through them the Spirit of Guidance pours blessings upon the world.

NOVEMBER 29

*The deeper your prayers echo in your own consciousness,
the more audible they are to God.*

God is in the depths of consciousness. Now the Message of God, being the Message of God, has employed such prayers as would make this a reality in one. The idea of words not carrying life is foreign to Sufism. Sufism is the philosophy of life, so its words must be living words. While it is not wrong to petition God, the training in Sufism enables one to pray in a practical manner to attain to Success. Saum, Salat, Khatum, and all prayers that have been included in any portion of the Sufi message given by Hazrat Inayat Khan are valuable beyond conception.

If it be supposed that one might petition God without these prayers, it is not wrong, but if one be a lover of another, the lover does not ask the beloved to assume tasks which the lover might do by oneself. Therefore, for the purpose of attainment it is preferable to practice meditation or concentration and not to petition God. We should rather pray by saying, "Use us for the purpose that Thy Wisdom chooses," and "Give sustenance to our bodies, hearts, and souls." Such a prayer combined with *Darood*, meditation, and concentration will serve every need of humanity.

NOVEMBER 30

*It is the depth of thought that is powerful,
and sincerity of feeling which creates atmosphere.*

The judgment of average people is based upon their own individual experience; the judgment of the wise is based upon the universal human experience. As one cannot tell what this universal experience is through the limited mind, one feels through impression by an inner attunement what this conclusion should be. So the heart tells one what the mind can never know off-hand, but which the mind may immediately grasp thereupon.

To keep the thought pure, therefore, the heart must be kept pure. Through concentration and meditation on unity in love the heart is purified and radiates its condition to all the world.

DECEMBER 1

The higher you rise, the wider becomes the margin of your view.

Mind can only see what it has experienced, but the mind of an intelligent person will consider what others have experienced. However, all the experience and knowledge of all people is beyond the ken of any one. This grand view is only possible to hold in the heart, which may be attuned to the whole universe. When one has love for all humankind, one can feel—even as a mother or father would— the condition of humankind, the need of humankind.

And one can extend this feeling to animal, plant, rock, and even beyond space and time and sphere as the heart expands. Extension of view increases capacity of heart, and increase of capacity of heart extends view. This is all caused by *Ishk* and is nothing but *Ishk*.

DECEMBER 2

*Justice can never be developed while we judge others;
the only way is by constantly judging ourselves.*

The reason is this: when one is called upon to be a judge, there should be no weights on either side of a balance. If two persons come to one for judgment, and there is a law book to be consulted, that law book would render judgment. But when one has no such reference or depends upon one's judgment, there is ordinarily no way to keep clear of prejudices which impede true justice.

By our judging ourselves is meant not so much a struggle against passion and evil, as a struggle from all influences be they good or bad. When one responds readily to the call of God from within, the heart and mind become purified from the denseness of the earth. This purification is the real judging of self, and not considering whether one's characteristics are good or bad or need to be removed or strengthened. Rather it is the judging of the *nufs*, the cause of all impurity. Judge that and not quality, and one in time will be able to render justice to oneself and another.

DECEMBER 3

Joy and sorrow are the light and shade of life;
without light and shade no picture is clear.

Joy produces light and at the same time joy is the result of light. Nothing stands in front of joy except the false concept of self. One can therefore escape both joy and sorrow by escaping concept.

Pictures are caused by variations in light and darkness, also in color. In true love there are no such variations. Mind is created in order that the soul might see life on the surface, and it is mind which has capacity for all lights and shades and colors. Therefore joy and sorrow are essentially conditions of mind. Pure-essence of mind does not know sorrow, which is caused by thought of self. Neither does it know joy although its condition is not different from what we call joy.

The reason that one experiences joy as joy is because it is differentiated from the condition when one feels sorrow and pain and difficulty. The realized soul no longer feels sorrow and pain and difficulty; consequently when one enters the higher states of consciousness one is no longer intoxicated by them, but understands them to be more natural than the ordinary state of life.

DECEMBER 4

The wise submit to conditions when they are helpless, bowing to the will of God, but
the evil that is avoidable they root out without sparing one single moment or effort.

Wise control of breath keeps the mind from lingering upon destructive thought. All destruction in the world is not evil, for sometimes it is necessary for the sake of all humankind or for the sake of earth itself. That is why there may be floods and droughts and even famine and pestilence. These universal conditions are the results of universal corruption.

But when the wise are called upon to oppose evil they do this immediately with all heart and mind, calling forth the power of God to work righteousness.

DECEMBER 5

Enviable is one who loveth and asketh no return.

It is only heart which can heal heart. When heart depends upon other than heart, heart has still to learn. The Sufi system of spiritual dependence upon a teacher is founded upon this principle, that when one's heart is not open, it can be awakened either by complete attunement with a being whose heart is already opened or who is attuning himself or herself to one whose heart is opened.

There is no asking or seeking in love—or giving or taking. The natural condition of heart is this: that when it loves others it feeds itself and when it feeds itself it shares with all others. This explains the mysteries of the loaves and fishes of the Bible. Loaves are the Divine Knowledge and the fishes symbolize the breath. No matter how much the Divine Knowledge is given away, it is not diminished; rather the more one shares with another, the more one benefits.

DECEMBER 6

To deny the changeableness of life is like fancying a motionless sea,
which can only exist in one's imagination.

Even the concept of *Nirvana* is not stillness. It is a ceaseless, rhythmical activity. Life is motion, love is motion, and light is motion. Stillness represents the condition of the cipher, *Nirvana* that of infinity. There can be no real idea of stillness because even conceiving stillness is an activity of mind. The control of mind activity through spiritual contemplation is an activity of heart and soul. The paralysis of mind through drugs or hypnotism is a chemical activity which disposes mind-activity in the first instance, and the activity of another's mind in the second instance. When the chemical forces abate or when the mind of another loses control, mind again functions.

The saying, "Nature abhors a vacuum," extends beyond the physical. It means that whenever there is a withdrawal there is a compensation elsewhere. It is only by force that force can be withdrawn; so even cessation of movement is dependent upon movement.

December 7

Learn to live a true life and you will know the truth.

Trueness comes from the attunement of heart, which is possible when the *nufs* is quieted. That is to say, when negation is negated, when falsehood is refuted, Truth comes to manifestation.

December 8

Wisdom is attained in solitude.

Wisdom is attained when the body is in solitude, which means that when the body is not overfed with earthly food, when it is not being used entirely for physical and mental labors, it becomes the temple of God.

Wisdom is attained when the mind is in solitude; that is to say, when the thoughts are no longer permitted to run at random, the light of intelligence may illuminate it.

Wisdom is attained in the solitude of heart; that is to say, when there is no love but love of God, when there is full dependence upon God and devotion to God, Wisdom is the natural result.

At the same time, Wisdom gives more scope to heart, mind, and body. This permits love for everybody or for anything, this inspires every type of mental and moral aspiration, and this gives the body such an education and stimulation that it may have a maximum of health and pleasure. In this there is no separation; it is the fulfillment of unity even in the outer life. By "solitude," living in oneness is meant—whether alone or in the crowd, whether in the desert or forest or city.

Mystics do leave inhabited places when the influences are too strong—and rightly. The need is to find God, and when anything interferes with this it is proper to withdraw from society.

DECEMBER 9

The seeming death of the body is the real birth of the soul.

By death of the body is meant dissolution, of course. For when this physical body is disintegrated, the soul is no longer a captive to time and space and its life becomes much more real.

In another sense, body means much more than just the physical body; any body—earth-body, mind-body, or even heart-body—seems to exact something from soul so that it does not fully realize its complete union and unity with God.

Again, death of body may mean death of the influence of body. This is a most wonderful process. When one has completely realized God while in the physical body, when one has attained to liberation, the form of the body remains—one still has a chemical body but there is a marvelous change in it. The old physical atoms fall away and are displaced by finer particles. These are more attenuated and are filled with the life-force which flows forth from the heart—not with the blood so much as around the blood like magnetism flows around an electric wire.

This living magnetism produces a living light and sometimes this light can manifest. Thus Jesus Christ has said, "Let your light shine before men." This light was also seen in Moses when the Glory of God shone upon him, and it is called *Kevod* by the Hebrews. This is the living breath and life of God. It is also manifested in Mohammed whose inner light was so great that sometimes he cast no shadow. It was this attainment which gave him the right to be called Mohammed. By Sufis the light of the whole manifest universe is called *Nuri Mohammed.*

This spiritual physical body is called *Nirmanakaya,* or body of transformation, by the Buddhists, and it can be dissolved instantly at what is called death. Such dissolution certainly was true in the historical cases of Moses, Elijah, Jesus Christ, Kabir, and many others. There is not always instantaneous dissolution because if the body is kept whole, or parts remain, they help to sanctify the earth. So Mohammed was placed in a tomb and the remains of Buddha placed in *stupas.*

December 10

As the rose blooms amidst thorns, so great souls shine out through all opposition.

There are two attitudes to take in the face of opposition: one is to oppose the enemy with all the power at your command. If by the use of force you are unable to win, force should not be used. The reason is not only because of success or failure, although this also is important. The reason is that it is necessary for you to change your own *nufs* and also the *nufs* of another. If in strife you break down the *nufs* of another, and if—when by the power of God vouchsafed to you—this can be done, it is not wrong to use force, and it never has been wrong to use such force. Every prophet has followed this path, and no one can become a prophet unless he or she will do so.

But there are subtler souls and also sometimes gentle people who cannot be reached this way. Conniving persons who use no force but depend upon cleverness must be combated in another way. It is not wrong to say that loving one's enemies and opposing them are necessarily different in action. In such cases, it is often wise to offer no resistance to evil. Then the enemy becomes like one rushing forward, not seeing the precipice over which they will fall.

There is another attitude to consider in offering no resistance to evil. This means to refuse to accept the opposition of another, to consider them not at all. This was the position of the Buddha, who overcame his enemies by refusing to recognize them physically, mentally, or spiritually. The result was that their thought could not cast any shadow over his mind. By this the Mahatma (that is to say, Buddha) shone through all the opposition. A shade, or physical obstacle, may block sunlight from a room but it cannot stop the sunlight.

December 11

When artists lose themselves in their art, then the art comes to life.

By this means God created the world, and partly in imitation of Allah it is wise to follow such a course. Metaphysically speaking there is another explanation. Energy and magnetism are imparted to us with breath. When the breath is used to praise God or is returned to God with fervor and remembrance, this increases the capacity for inspiration. In every form of inspiration—whether one understands it spiritually or not—all interest is focused in one's work. Then the divine breath touches every portion of one's being and this passes into the form which the artist is shaping—be one a musician, poet, architect, artisan, or any other molder of beauty.

DECEMBER 12

Do not anything with fear; and fear not whatever you do.

Fear is the time for inaction, for sedation, for meditation. This is true physically as well as spiritually. Fear interferes with breath and at the same time fear is the result of a defect in breath. To guard against fear, Sufis are trained in self-protection, first through *Darood*, then in Occultism, which enables one to overcome all fear and to face all conditions.

Likewise, all acts should be done with full faith and without questioning their outcome. Otherwise, it is better to abstain from action. For this also, one gains through *Darood*, which makes God the actor. Standing by one's actions, one brings moral magnetism into them and gives them life and power, and at the same time acting in this way helps the devotee.

DECEMBER 13

Love develops into harmony, and of harmony is born beauty.

If there were an opposite condition to Love, it would not be hate, but chaos. Hate is a force derived from love, concentrated through *nufs*. Chaos, on the other hand, is the opposite of all love. Allah, through *Ishk*, destroyed and destroys chaos, and the first sign of the absence of chaos is the music of life expressed in rhythms and harmonies. This is the cause of all vibrations, out of which all worlds were made.

Beauty is the natural result of harmony in that it uplifts the soul. The harmonies, melodies, and rhythms of vibrations and forms are intoxicating. One can see in an instant the inspiration of an artist; one can see that one picture does not inspire and another does inspire the witness. Beauty in form, be it in nature or from human hands, is always compelling and uplifting.

DECEMBER 14

One who keeps no secrets has no depth in his or her heart.

The tongue brings all life to the surface and keeps life on the surface. When one is silent, particularly in *Darood*, the life force touches the deepest parts of one's being. When one has something to say and does not say it except to whisper it (so to speak) to God, that thing is endowed with life and blessing, and if it is a wish, verily will it be fulfilled. If it is a danger to another, verily another will be protected when one keeps the secret in silence, whispering only to God.

DECEMBER 15

Behind us all is one spirit and one life;
how then can we be happy if our neighbor is not also happy?

Happiness is the condition of the heart. Heart touches every other heart. What is wished in the heart is wished for all persons or is not wished. That is the test of wish in the head or in the heart. A *Bodhisattva* does not cease wishing; rather *Bodhisattva's* wishes are for all humanity. This shows the nature of heart, which cannot and does not discriminate.

Can the unhappiness of another dull one's spirit? No, sympathy does not mean to let the shadow of another fall upon one's being; it is to let one's light bring life to another. Spiritual gifts must be shared or they will be taken away from one, for they are for all of God's children and not for a favored few.

DECEMBER 16

The sea of life is in constant motion; no one can stop its ever-moving waves.
The Masters walk over the waves, the wise swim in the water,
but the ignorant are drowned in their effort to cross.

Here we have three degrees of evolution. The ignorant do not use their mind, although sometimes they may let their mind use them. They do not think steadily or regularly and are like a straw blown in the wind. They are more affected by opinion than by thought and want to go with the majority. They do not and cannot comprehend their own duties in life and are bound to failure.

To help such people, one must treat them as children even when offering respect due to age or position. Nevertheless, they must be considered inwardly as children and not treated too harshly when they would not understand; neither should they be treated too lightly when no impression would therefore be made. They may be permitted to feel that they have their own way, yet they are to be controlled at all times. The spiritual person becoming negative to such people is in grave danger.

The wise are ones who use their mind, who control their mind. For this, will-power is necessary. Such people may not be endowed with great insight but will be strong enough to battle their way in life. There are sometimes mental and moral giants that have enough capabilities to withstand the struggles of life without being overcome by them. Yet they are quite unable to lead others out of the morass.

It is such souls who are ready for the Message, but also such souls may not see the need of the Message. When they are intuitive they escape much of the turmoil of life and by leading their own selves are often able to lead others.

Masters are those whose hearts do control mind and body, who entertain no diversity of opinions, and who do not depend upon others for their thoughts unless they recognize the others' authority. They do not claim to be all-wise for they are just as cognizant of their limitations as they are aware of God's All-Embracing Power. Such people may not be controllers of others or of affairs, but they will be able to stand where they want to stand. They will be able to cover their course in life, and they will not be deterred by earthly conditions for they have arisen above the state where they would be affected by them.

DECEMBER 17

Our greatest privilege is to become a suitable instrument of God.

Nothing is more beautiful than the vision of God. But nothing is more noble than to let God see visions out of one's eyes, so that God may look upon the world and serve the world and give the world all the succor it needs. This is self-sacrifice, which is sacrifice only of limitation and selfishness and brings one infinite capacity.

DECEMBER 18

The trees of the forest silently await God's blessing.

The Hebrew people have an article of faith that reads: "I believe with perfect faith in the coming of the Messiah, and though he may tarry, yet I will await his coming." Now the law of the Universe is that patience itself enables one to receive the blessing of God, for by that one escapes all the emotions which hamper one at every turn.

If human beings are wiser than the vegetable we must lead a wiser life, and we cannot do that until we learn all the wisdom from the lower creation. Every virtue of every rock, plant, or animal can be cultivated and perfected in us. In the inner life, one often has to develop the qualities one finds in nature, and it is the development of these qualities which bring perfection. Self-surrender is not an annihilation—nothing is destroyed, but the shadow-thought of self is turned into light, and all the qualities accumulated by the soul are brought to perfection.

DECEMBER 19

The plain truth is too simple for the seekers after complexity,
who are looking for things they cannot understand.

The emotional stir of things and the intoxication of the outer life are the great detriments. One who has become accustomed to them grows to love complexities. Now heart is not complex although heart may be considered as "involved." That is to say, one cannot by simple analysis find heart. Heart is simple but not analyzable. One cannot express the greater in terms of the smaller and still understand the greater. The human being is an aggregate of cells, let us say. Yet we can study physical cells forever and never discover the human. This shows there is something missing in analysis.

That there is something missing in analysis every little child knows—as well as a loving mother and a kind father, often quite involuntarily—for it is the very nature of life that causes them to feel this something. This is *Ishk*, the great life-force of the Universe which is tendered to everyone through Divine Guidance.

DECEMBER 20

Unsuccessful ones often keep success away
by the impression of their former failures.

Failure is due to wrong direction of breath. Concentration improves breath, especially spiritual concentration. Every thought affects the breath very appreciably. So by your impressions you can move your breath and so alter condition of mind and body. Thinking about failures is sure to increase failure, and thinking of success will surely bring success in some direction. Therefore you are the cause of your own miseries.

DECEMBER 21

We ourselves are the tree of desire, and the root of that tree is in our own heart.

Human beings from the very beginning feel a longing. We seek satisfaction for that longing in life—in our incarnation, in marriage, in bringing forth children, and in many common pursuits—but never does one find satisfaction until one's longing returns to the heart from which it first came.

DECEMBER 22

With good will and trust in God, self-confidence,
and a hopeful attitude towards life,
one can always win one's battle, however difficult.

When there is trust in God, there can be no defeat. When one is bound by one's conception of God, when one limits God by one's human conception, one's trust is necessarily limited. To increase the scope of trust one must find a greater being in whom to trust, and if this being is limited by human thought, then trust is limited. Besides, a person who has not trusted his or her human kin does not know the meaning of trust. How can such a one trust in God?

The Sufis, beginning with God, placing God beyond conception, put all their trust in the Living Reality, then assure themselves of that trust and faith and by it are able to overcome all difficulties.

No one is unable to do this; the Spirit of Guidance within will lead one forth from every discomfort. This proves the great wisdom of God.

Sufis, through their spiritual exercises, remove the path and shadow of *nufs* which always hinders success.

DECEMBER 23

There are many paths, and each one of us considers our own the best and wisest. Let each one of us choose that which belongs to our own temperament.

In the spiritual life, it is not necessary to change one's occupation or livelihood. The doctor may remain a doctor, the artisan may continue as an artisan, the farmer must till the soil, the merchant may keep in business, and the laborer needs to continue at the job. Oftentimes one changes one's pursuit; this is right if one has not been in a position to attain one's ideal at work. But it is wrong to change the ideal. Retain the ideal and attain it.

One should neither advise others to change their direction in life nor turn from one's own path. This is the maxim of the wise, and it holds whether it is change or continuance of pursuit that leads to God. While the God-ward path is the right path, to each one of us is allotted the particular path best for us. In uniformity there is no music; there is harmony when every one of us can find happiness in our own ideal.

DECEMBER 24

Failure, either in health or affairs, means there has been lack of self-control.

Nufs is unable to direct affairs. *Nufs* has no wisdom, and cannot see ahead. *Nufs* urges one to eat delicious food but sees no illness resulting. *Nufs* caters to passions and does not recognize weakness until too late. *Nufs* surrenders to vice and puts the blame elsewhere. A person under the sway of *nufs* seldom attains success and quickly loses the greatest success no matter what pain and sacrifice were undergone in the attainment.

Self-control surely wins success in the end, for body, mind, and heart follow the true course. By it, one shapes the mind first and the destiny afterwards. That is true freedom of Will which achieves success in relation to the ideal.

DECEMBER 25

Love is as the water of the Ganges; it is in itself a purification.

Heart heals heart. Heart may contract or expand. Heart's expansion is caused by *Ishk* which brings healing and joy, and this joy touches every corner of the Universe. The lover is as the sun which radiates energy everywhere. This cannot be explained. It is the nature of love, it is the quality of *Ishk*, it is the *Sifat*, or divine quality, of God.

DECEMBER 26

Love is unlimited, but it needs scope to expand and rise;
without that scope life is unhappy.

Involution is really involution of love or *Ishk*. An accommodation was made which produced mind. Through mind, soul could see the physical plane. But mind also created thoughts, which proved confusing. Love does not think, yet understands thought. Love hampered by thought cannot rise and expand. Love, free from the bondage of self, can expand or contract without hindrance and without confusion. These stages of the heart are experienced by the mystics and form the spiritual life.

DECEMBER 27

Every wave of the sea, as it rises, seems to be stretching its hands upwards,
as if to say, "Take me higher and higher."

The waves of the sea are partly caused by the tides, which are the result of gravitation, which in turn is an activity of *Ishk* in the physical sphere. This movement upward of the water, whether as wave or as vapor, is caused by the law that to find liberation one must become other than what one has been. So the water becomes the vapor and the vapor the cloud. Yet the *nufs* of water is such that the emancipation does not make water non-water.

So human emancipation does not make one other than human; one can become neither animal nor angel, though one behave worse than animal or better than angel. There is a ceaseless striving in every form, and the seeking of liberation is the seeking of God.

DECEMBER 28

True pleasure lies in the sharing of joy with another.

As the loaves and fishes of Christ increased in division, so the joys of life grow more abundant when shared. In reality, sharing is the joy and not sharing the sorrow of life. If one shares and shares, one will find more and more joy, being freed from earthly attachment. This is the true wealth of life, which is not conditioned by any plane of existence.

DECEMBER 29

A gain or loss which is momentary is not real; if we knew realities we should never grieve over the loss of anything which experience shows to be only transitory.

The human being is greater than anything in the physical or mental world. One cannot take the wealth of this world into *Malakut*, and all of *Malakut* is one's possession when one enters *Djabrut*. We understand when leaving this world we cannot carry away its possessions, but we can carry thoughts and these thoughts deter the pilgrim in the higher life.

The human being is a mirror which reflects all things in the worlds above or below. The *sahib-i-dil*, knowing this, do not have to accumulate knowledge. They see what they need reflected in mind, be that knowledge from the worlds above or below. This is a great wonder incomprehensible to average people. Yet the sage attaches no value to the faculty. Soul sees because it sees and when no longer confined to a narrow sphere by mind, all gains and losses pass away. In the infinite are all things.

December 30

A soul is as great as the circle of its influence.

When the soul depends upon physical wealth and possessions, it touches only those who are controlled or influenced by wealth and possessions. When the soul longs for fame, it gains only the respect of those who respect fame or power. When the soul develops intellectual genius, it carries a possession beyond this sphere, which is of great value in *Malakut* and which helps the souls coming toward manifestation and many on their return journey. Besides, it influences the mental atmosphere of earth and so aids the people to acquire still greater mental capacity and genius. This all helps in the experience of life.

Still greater is the scope of heart and the advantage that results from the spiritual life. For only the spiritual ones can discern causes and purposes, and they do not have to explain. They know explanations are of no value to those who have never loved, and that those who love need no explanation. The heart, being greater than mind, can perceive every function of mind. Therefore the seers may read the mind of another and gain the knowledge of another, but they consider mind in its proper place. The *sahib-i-dil*, the keepers of the heart, are therefore not limited by human ability or power or wealth or intellect or memory. Their influence extends into *Djabrut*, touches all three planes, and extends into the future on earth and heaven.

Still greater yet is the influence of one who has accomplished the spiritual journey and become *Rassoul*. There is no end to the circle of the *Rassoul's* influence, which is eternal.

December 31

Happiness lies in thinking or doing that which one considers beautiful.

Purest selfishness ends in unselfishness. Selfish people never entirely satisfy themselves. And when they ultimately do find a way to satisfy themselves, it entails satisfying others. This shows that all roads lead to God. Beauty is the desire of every soul and beauty is the essence of the Personality of God.

About the Cover Design

"The Bowl of Saki" is a divine message from above of perennial, timeless, and poetical expression. The height, breadth, and depth of the message within "The Bowl of Saki" touch the very heart of our humanity. Its language is an intricate pattern of exquisitely interwoven expressions and revelations that have the capacity to instill awe, wonder, and nourishment on the unfolding path of spiritual awakening in everyday life. All this has been contemplated in the selection of the design elements for this special text. The cover photo, by Pir Shabda Kahn, is a fragment of the dome of the largest mosque in Europe, found in Saint Petersburg, Russia. The domed mosaic is intended to express an intricacy of interconnectedness; both overarching and enveloping, while reaching out to touch the reader. It is an invitation to enter the sacred space. ~ *Professor Nuria Stephanie Sabato*

28907896R00115